Falcons' Flight

Linda Linton

Order this book online at www.trafford.com
or email orders@trafford.com

Most Trafford titles are also available at major online book retailers.

Print information available on the last page.

ISBN: 978-1-5521-2649-3 (sc)
ISBN: 978-1-4122-4297-4 (e)

Trafford rev. 12/13/2022

www.trafford.com

North America & international
toll-free: 844-688-6899 (USA & Canada)
fax: 812 355 4082

For my family,
With love

ACKNOWLEDGMENTS

I would like to express my deep appreciation to those who helped make this work possible.

First and foremost, I am grateful to my parents for their openness, their support and their patience with me throughout these ten years from our trip to Bermuda until this manuscript was completed for their 60th wedding anniversary and throughout the publishing process.

I would also like to recognize the contributions of Carol Cadmus and Lucy Straus for their editorial expertise, Mildred Coté for layout, and Tom Ricotta for the cover design.

A special thanks to Ned McLeod and Malinda Lugo for their legal advice and moral support. And my heartfelt gratitude to Margaret Devenny and the Trafford staff for facilitating the smooth launch of *Falcons' Flight*.

And finally, I'd like to thank my Vic, for his love and his belief in me.

AUTHOR'S NOTE

While this memoir is based on real characters and historical events, some of the names and situations have been altered to accommodate discrepancies among individual recollections, to protect personal privacy and to enhance the flow of the story.

The photographs, exclusive of the family portrait and the wedding day photo, were all taken by Alfred (Liebermann) Linton during the journey described in this book.

Linda Linton

PROLOGUE

On a beautiful July weekend in 1988, my family gathered at a hotel in Hamilton, Bermuda, for an extraordinary experience. My parents invited my sister, my brother, their spouses and children, my boyfriend and me to join them on this lovely island. The gathering was planned, ostensibly, to celebrate my parents' 50th wedding anniversary. For three days we played on the beaches, toured the island, and enjoyed one another's company as we basked in the sun.

But what transpired every evening as we assembled in my parents' hotel room affected each of us profoundly. For three consecutive nights, my father and mother told us about the past 50 years of their lives.

As I began to listen to the stories that unfolded that first evening in Hamilton, I realized that for nearly 35 years I had had no idea of the hardships my parents had endured to arrive in America.

My father had chosen Hamilton as the place to reveal their tale because it was the first harbor in the "New World" where he and Mom had landed after their long ordeal of running from the Nazis. As we were to discover, however, the landing in Bermuda was by no means a safe ending to their journey.

50th Wedding Anniversary Family Portrait

Linda Linton

INTRODUCTION

July 2, 1988
Somewhere over the Atlantic Ocean

Gazing out the window en route to Bermuda, my eyes lost focus and I stared down onto what appeared to be armfuls of white cotton candy. I love to fly. The temporary separation from the chaos and daily stresses of the world below always gives me the feeling of great freedom and peace. It's as though I've been given permission to let go for a while, to loosen the desperate grip on the controls governing the minute details of my life. And in those blissful moments of abandonment, I reflected on the preparations for this trip and wondered what the next few days would bring.

My Dad had planned every detail meticulously. He wanted this celebration of their 50th wedding anniversary to be just the way he liked things best: with the family gathered around. It's funny. In some ways, our family is not what an outsider would call "close knit." We all live within about a 100-mile radius of Mom and Dad's house in Philadelphia, but we get together only a few times a year, on Thanksgiving, Christmas, and maybe a birthday or two. My older sister, Sue, and her husband and two boys live in the Poconos. My brother John and his wife, together with their two children are in the Philadelphia suburbs of Bucks County. Then there's me, Linda, the youngest, living in New Jersey near the shore.

For this celebration, we could have met at Mom and Dad's house with less than a two-hour drive. Yet here we were, all of us flying to an island resort to spend four days together at the South Hampton Princess Hotel in Hamilton, Bermuda. This was definitely a very special occasion.

The clouds began to part like white silk scarves flung aside by some magician, revealing jewels of blue topaz and turquoise sparkling in the ocean below. Tiny dots became tinker-toy-sized sailboats, and as the plane swung in a wide circle over the water, the coral pink island of Bermuda came into view.

Dad had everything set up. During the day we could do as we wished on our own. We could go to the beach, sightsee, play golf. Dinner would be together, of course.

And then, Dad explained, he wanted everyone to gather in his and mom's room after dinner each evening to talk. This part of the trip had us intrigued. We weren't exactly sure what we would talk about, but Dad had even suggested we bring tape recorders. He said he wanted to tell all of us, the children and the grandchildren, the story of what had happened over the past 50 years.

You have to understand that this was a pretty remarkable concept. In our family we didn't often talk about the past. Johnny and Susie and I had heard only bits and pieces of stories over the years. We knew that our parents had met in Brussels, Mom's hometown, around the time of World War II. We knew that Mom's family was Catholic and Dad's family was Jewish. And we all knew that Dad was born in Vienna and that the rest of his family had fled Austria and reached America long before Mom and Dad arrived here. I remember hearing the story of how one of my uncles had chosen our new family name (changing it from Liebermann, a name that was both German and Jewish) to make it "more American." My uncle chose the name merely by opening the telephone book to the "L's" and pointing to a name at random. That name turned out to be Linton.

But except for those few tiny scraps of information, the early part of Mom and Dad's relationship had never been discussed. They didn't even teach us their native languages, French and German. Mom did sing some French songs to us when we were very little—I remember learning to sing "Sur le Pont d'Avignon." And when we visited our aunts and uncles, the grownups would often speak German, so I did learn to understand a little. But whenever I asked why they didn't teach us German or French, Mom would say, "If you want to learn another language, you must go to the country where it is spoken." They wanted us to be 100 percent American kids, with an American name and America's language.

So none of us had any idea of the adventure story we were about to hear.

CHAPTER 1

July 3, 1988
Hamilton Harbor, Bermuda

It had been a beautiful day and we'd all had a chance to enjoy the beach for a while. After indulging in a delicious dinner served in the French restaurant near the hotel, we all settled down in "Nanny and Papa's room" as the grandchildren would say. My boyfriend grabbed a chair and I found a comfortable spot on the floor in front of him . The children sprawled on the beds while their parents slid into the remaining chairs and propped their feet up on the beds. Those of us with tape recorders flipped them on. Then we all focused our attention on my Dad.

"Everybody's having a good time and that's wonderful," he began. "That's the way we planned it. And we thought this would be a perfect time to talk, with the whole family together. We'll talk about our background, which means, in turn, that it's your background, too. Today, we have an ideal opportunity to tell you about how our family began. I picked Bermuda for this occasion, not only because it's a wonderful place and not too far from America, but also because it has been a true turning point in our lives–that is, Nanny's and mine- from a sort of Hell, to a Free World. And that happened right here in Hamilton Harbor."

"So let's start at the beginning. Since I'm the oldest, we'll start with my beginning."

"I was born on March 14, 1915, in the apartment of my parents in Vienna, Austria. It was just the beginning of the First World War. I was named Alfred Ernst Liebermann. Liebermann was our family name."

And he went on to tell us about his early childhood. He told us about Grandpop, Norbert Liebermann, and Grandmom, Leontine, who was called Tina. He told us about his brother, our Uncle Otto, and his two sisters, our Aunt Erna and Aunt Olga.

In 1920 when he was five years old, my father and his sisters were sent by train to

Denmark, along with many hundreds of children. (Their little brother, who was three years old at the time, was considered too young for the trip.) They were sent away because the conditions in postwar Vienna were severe. Food was very scarce and parents were struggling to keep their families alive. When conditions improved, the children returned to Vienna to be reunited with their families.

"I stayed for a year with loving foster parents in Hinnerup, Denmark," my father continued. "Upon my return home to Vienna, I went to school. First I attended elementary school, then middle school.

"At that time, your Grandpop, my father, was involved in the Vienna municipal organization. He ran an insurance company that was owned and supervised by the city of Vienna.

"Our family was a typical Viennese middle class family of Jewish ancestry," my dad went on. "We were a non-practicing Jewish family because in Austria, even today, religion is very unimportant and does not play an important part in public life, but does in private life. And nobody interfered with anyone else's private life. You couldn't tell who was Catholic or Jewish or Protestant. That was considered private. In fact, we had the option, in Austria, to state officially that we were "Konfessionslos," which meant you have no formalized religious affiliation. As a young adult in Vienna, I chose to be listed in this way."

While I listened to my father describing the attitudes about religion in Austria, I reflected on my own experience when I chose to join the Presbyterian Church as a teenager. I recalled that my parents allowed us all to make our own decisions regarding our personal religious affiliations. I also remember that neither of my parents was particularly enthusiastic about discussing personal religious issues at home. I was now beginning to understand why that subject might have made them uncomfortable.

My dad's voice became stronger as he went on to describe other aspects of his life in Austria.

"Our political position was a different story," he said. " We were very aware of the politics of that time and we became personally involved in the community. My father was an active member of the Socialist party of Austria, and I was influenced at a young age by his activities.

"The Social Democrats have been running Austria ever since the First World War and doing a wonderful job. The Social Democratic Party is Socialist, not Communist. It's very progressive. Things are done for the people, for all the people. And the Austrian Social Democratic Party has been a role model for the world."

At this point, Dad took us back to his own active political role and the dangers he faced.

"As a young boy, I joined a Social Democratic Youth group. This group was like the

Falcons' Flight

Boy Scouts, except that it was mixed boys and girls. I was initiated by a well-known educator in Austria. After two years of active membership in my local district, I was asked to create a new group of my own. This new group was a subdivision of the Rote Falken, *which means Red Falcons in English."*

Dad went on to tell us about his friendship with the leader of all the Rote Falken *in Vienna. Dad would participate in meetings held in the leader's office at the fire department. As a leader himself, my father organized events and summer camps and managed the "photo Hut." Because he played the violin, he was in charge of the music activities as well.*

"When I began to go to 'Gymnasium', which was the name given to the next level of school after middle school," Dad explained, *"I attended the one that was in my section of Vienna, Währing. But, because of my political activities, I soon began to encounter hostilities from fellow classmates. So my parents had me transferred to a school in the fifth district to finish my studies.*

"I didn't do too well in high school," Dad confessed, *"so, I finally got a job as a clerk in an insurance company.*

"During that time, my activities with the Social Democratic Youth group made me a target of the Fascists when they came to power. I was stopped and searched by the police on many occasions. They were very, very nasty and mean.

"Realizing what a danger it was for me to remain in Austria," he said, *"my father contacted his friend who was the General Manager of the Belgian Insurance Company, 'La Prévoyance Sociale.' Together, they arranged for me to go to Belgium to work under this man's son, who was a division manager in Brussels.*

"I had only a few French lessons before my departure for Belgium." Dad continued. *But I quickly learned to speak French once I arrived. I spent much of my time in my new job translating correspondence in French and German between management in Brussels and provincial representation in the border area of Eupen-Malmedie (a Belgian province on the German border).*

"So, even though I was in a foreign country, speaking a foreign language," Dad told us, *"at least I was safe from the Austrian Fascists. Soon after settling down in Brussels, I joined a group called the 'Friends of Nature' along with fellow employees of the insurance company. And before long, I made other contacts which led me to become a member of* Les Faucons Rouges, *the sister group to the* Rote Falken. *"*

And with that vivid description of the early years, my father, and then my mother, went on to tell us the startling stories we had never heard before. As I sat wide-eyed with anticipation listening to the sound of their voices recounting their adventures, this is how I imagined it must have been....

CHAPTER 2

May 1, 1936
Brussels, Belgium

Alfred drew in a long slow breath. The crisp air of early May felt cool and refreshing. The sun was getting stronger, making him squint as he surveyed the wooded area where several young people were beginning to gather. He always enjoyed these Sunday outings, hiking and picnicking in the park with his friends. It wasn't exactly the mossy green beauty of the Vienna Woods where he had spent so much time as a boy. But for the attractive single man who had just turned 23, Brussels wasn't a bad place to be on a spring morning in 1936.

Alfred Liebermann, or Fredo, as his friends liked to call him, had been in Belgium less than two years. Yet already he spoke French like a native *"Brusseloix."* Because of his experience as a leader of the Social Democratic Youth organization in Vienna called *Rote Falken* or Red Falcons, it hadn't taken him long to become a leader of a similar group, *Les Faucons Rouges* here in Brussels. He had a sort of easygoing charm and felt very comfortable as the center of attention. And those dark brown eyes with just a hint of mischief added to his charisma, especially with the ladies.

"Eh, Fredo! There's a letter here for you," shouted one member of the group.

Alfred opened the envelope with care, noting that the postmark was from Pressburg, a city in Czechoslovakia. A quick glance at the end of the letter revealed the sender, John Hirschfeld.

"Merde," he thought, "those fascists in Austria are reading and censoring everything now. What possible interest could they have in a letter from my sister's boyfriend, that he had to go over the border to Pressburg to mail it?"

Alfred sat down under a tree and began to read. John described in great detail the arrest and beating of Otto, Alfred's brother, the youngest of the four Liebermann children.

Falcons' Flight

The police had come looking for Alfred for the third time. In their frustration at not finding the "troublemaking anti-Fascist boy" who was leading the *Rote Falken*, they arrested his brother instead. They beat Otto severely and then threw him into jail for two horrifying nights.

"Your father had to use his 'connections,' as always, to get Otto out of jail," John explained.

"If my father did not have the influential position at the *Wiener Städtische*, who knows what might have happened to my brother," Fredo thought.

Alfred's father had become a prominent individual in Vienna. The *Wiener Städtische Versicherung* (the insurance company for the City of Vienna) had hired Norbert Liebermann to help make a kind of dream for Vienna become reality. That dream was to establish a successful Viennese company and then utilize some of its profits to provide much-needed services to the people of the city. As General Manager of the insurance company for the city, *Herr Liebermann* had managed to provide hundreds of thousands of people with badly needed insurance, while using some of the profits of the company to build low-income housing and new fire department stations for the city. He was well respected and made a substantial living during a time when Vienna was a thriving center of European culture and commerce.

"You must not write to us or to your friends any longer, Alfred," John's letter went on. "Several of your recent correspondences have been intercepted by the authorities and they have gotten your friends into serious trouble. One of those friends, Josef, was arrested for high treason!"

"Na, so was! Now what!" Fredo exclaimed under his breath, slipping back into his native German as he went on to read the rest of the news from home. He could read between the lines. There was a growing fear of the ever-present police and the influence of Hitler's Nazi organization from Germany.

John wrote of Alfred's sister, Erna (John's girlfriend), who was being harassed at her sewing shop and was in fear of being chased out entirely by the militant Austro-fascists and Nazi sympathizers. John implied that he was looking for a way to travel with Erna to the United States. Several of his family members who now lived near New York had been urging them to get away from the encroaching dangers.

"And your sister Olga has her own problems, with a young son and no husband," the letter continued.

After her brief marriage ended in divorce, Olga had begun to practice law as part of the Courts in Vienna.

"She, too, is looking for a way out of Austria. Certainly she will not be able to practice law for much longer under these conditions."

Alfred wondered what "these conditions" really meant–although he was afraid he knew all too well. He had heard and read about the ways in which the Fascists had begun to force themselves into every aspect of the lives of the people in Austria. People whose philosophies differed even slightly from the dictatorial mandates of the Fascist government were watched, even stalked and persecuted. They were stripped of their money, their jobs, their possessions and often they were arrested. There were even rumors of public beatings and of women being raped.

Alfred hoped Mama was all right. As he leaned back and closed his eyes momentarily, he was transported in his mind from the wooded area outside Brussels to his home at Severin Schreibergasse, Number 27, in the 18th District of Vienna.

He could picture Mama working hard, as always, carrying groceries up the many concrete steps that led from the street below up to the pavement in front of their home. When Papa would come home, Mama would always have a good meal on the table for the family. And Alfred, who didn't eat very much anyway, would rush to finish supper so he could run out to meet his friends. He was always involved with some group of youngsters in the neighborhood. Alfred seemed to draw strength from the social interaction.

When he was only 11 years old, Alfred became a member of *Kinderfreunde*–Friends of the Children. It was an organization that was part of the Social Democratic Party. The group operated in schools and vacation homes throughout Austria and it was the "in group" for young people. It was a mixture of girls and boys who went hiking together on Sundays, with social and educational activities such as dancing and learning songs. It all seemed so innocent and lovely then.

As a young man of 14, Alfred was bright and talented–although you wouldn't know that from his performance at the *Gymnasium* (the Austrian equivalent of high school). He did, however, have a knack for pulling everyone together and giving them direction. He was a natural leader. And when he was encouraged to start a new subgroup of the *Rote Falken* in his Viennese neighborhood, it was a great success. In many ways, the *Rote Falken* was kind of a grown-up version of the *Kinderfreunde* and Alfred was instantly comfortable with the young adolescents with whom he went hiking and dancing, as he had with the younger group.

Only things were not so sweet and innocent any longer. Ever since that fateful day in 1927 when the world learned of the guilty verdict in the Sacco/Vanzetti trial, the political climate in Vienna had changed drastically. There were uprisings of sympathetic Socialists and union members worldwide who felt that Sacco and Vanzetti died martyrs to the causes of Justice and Freedom. In Vienna, there was a General Strike…a military confrontation… a horrendous fire that destroyed the Justice Palace… Hundreds of people were massacred all over Austria.

Suddenly the quiet, innocent get-togethers of teenagers became secret meetings and militant actions plotted against those followers of Mussolini and Dolfuss, the Austrian leader, who were growing more and more powerful against the Social Democrats in Austria. In school, Alfred had joined the militant Socialist students' organization, *Sozialistische Mittel-schüler und Studenten*. And even after high school, as he was an insurance company clerk, Alfred was leading militant actions against the Austro-Fascists.

Although Alfred's father supported his activities in principle, Norbert Liebermann clearly saw the impending dangers for his young activist son and arranged for him to flee the country and take refuge in an insurance company in Belgium until the danger had passed.

So, on July 23, 1934, the day that Chancellor Dolfuss was buried, having been assassinated by the dual forces of the Nazis and the militant fascists, Alfred had set out for Belgium. Little did he know then that he would soon be leading the Belgian version of the *Rote Falken* in Brussels.

Snapping himself back into the present, Alfred finished reading John's letter and stuffed it into his pocket. He allowed himself the luxury of a moment of homesickness and a passionate desire to see his family and friends in Vienna. Then he gathered himself up and joined his companions who were already greeting the other members of *Les Faucons Rouges*.

Alfred was not going to let thoughts of the potential dangers back home ruin this beautiful day. It was, after all, the first of May 1936. He was sharing the day with his Belgian companions and he had something rather special planned.

Linda Linton

CHAPTER 3

July 3, 1988
Bermuda

Just as we were becoming totally immersed in Dad's story of his first few years in Belgium, he paused and turned to Mom and asked her to tell us a little bit about her own background.

"Why didn't you discuss this with me first?" she asked, feeling slightly uneasy with the spotlight now pointed at her.

"Because I always surprise you!" Dad responded, with a devilish glint in his eye.

It then became very clear that our father, always a bit dramatic and often hesitant to let anyone else know what he was up to, had not explained to Mom what would take place during their Golden Wedding anniversary celebration in Bermuda with the family.

Mom hesitated and stared at Dad for a moment. Awkwardly wondering where to begin, she tried to break the ice with a joke:

"Should I say that in Belgium all the babies are born in cabbage patches?!"

Smiles and giggles around the room broke the tension. For a moment I remembered how, when I was a little girl, my mother had told me there were no storks in Belgium. So, the children were told that babies came from cabbage patches.

Mom then took a deep breath and began:

"I was born in 1920 in Brussels, during the depression. My full name is Laure Marie Gislaine Deprince. My father, Maurice, worked for the railroad. We were very poor. I had a brother who came four years after me, Roger, and then another when I was 13, that's Uncle Jacques.

"I was raised a Catholic, because 98 percent of the people in Belgium are Catholic. My mother, Juliette, was very broad-minded about religion. She felt her duty was to

baptize us, and make sure we were confirmed. Then, when we were about 14, we could decide what we wanted to do. That's when I decided to stop going to church."

Mom went on to tell us many other details about her childhood. She told us she had been a sickly child, prone to terrible bouts of chronic bronchitis nearly every winter. The tiny, cold apartment her family lived in was barely large enough to accommodate the four of them when it was just Mom and her brother Roger. But when the third child, Jacques, was born, the crowded two-room flat became nearly intolerable.

They didn't have running water, so Grandmom (my grandmother) had to carry clean water up the stairs and waste water back down the stairs every day. There was one toilet located downstairs in a common area. They had a coal burning stove, which barely gave off enough heat to quell the cold and dampness of the Belgian climate. It was no wonder that Grandmom sent Mom to visit her Aunt Leontine in the country each summer, hoping the fresh air would clear her lungs of the bronchitis.

Besides bouts of illness, Mom struggled with very low self-esteem. Her father paid little, if any, attention to her. He often came home drunk and erupted in loud and even violent arguments with her mother. Since he spent much of the meager wages he earned on liquor, he never had any money to spend on necessities or treats for his children. And he had no interest in spending time talking with them, or giving them the affection they craved.

So Mom found solace in romance novels and classics like Les Misérables that she borrowed from her friend, Louisette. She loved to read and she earned very good grades, even though she didn't really study very hard. She had completed the required eight grades with ease. She would like to have studied art, but her mother had insisted she take the boring sewing classes offered at the Art School, L'École des Arts de la Ville de Bruxelles.

So, soon after she reached age 14, when leaving school was permitted under Belgian law, our mother quit school and took a job to help support her family. She was painfully shy and very self-conscious about her appearance, especially her many freckles. And she desperately wanted to be accepted, particularly by the boys.

She was also extremely sensitive and observant, noticing everything and everyone, including the young man in her group of friends who was from Austria and spoke French with a Brussels accent.

"Did you like him?" my sister asked her.

"Yes, I always liked the new boys in the group," was her response.

At this point, we were all expecting to hear our mother relate the story of how she met Dad–"a love-at-first-sight story." But, she surprised us by describing her first trip away from home, and another young man who had captured her attention. As Mom began telling us about the field trip to Paris, I could envision the whole scene.

Linda Linton

❧❧❧

August 1935
Somewhere in France

The train was speeding through the French countryside. The 10:55 from Paris to Brussels had arrived precisely on time, as the trains in Europe invariably did. It was one of those things that you could always count on.

For the young girl slumped in the last section of the third car, a punctual train was precisely what she had not desired. All she had wished for on that bleak summer day was to stand on the railroad platform forever, drinking in the sound of Etienne's voice, the feel of his hand in hers.

Laure Marie Deprince, or Laurette as her friends called her, was a gangling 14-year-old girl. She had strawberry-blond hair, and freckles that covered her whole face, her arms, and her legs, as if God had lost control of the "freckle shaker" while sprinkling her nose and spattered freckles everywhere. She had steely gray-green eyes that nearly always glowed with a flirtatious sparkle that belied her young years. Today, however, the sparkle slipped out of her eyes and slid down her cheek in several large teardrops.

It was her first time away from home. She had been to a large retreat of young Social Democrats from all over Europe, including her native Brussels. They had spent ten days listening to speeches, studying some of the customs and the cultural, and political issues they shared with France, and socializing with their newfound friends. One of the speakers had been the Prime Minister of France, Leon Blum. It had been a great experience-- especially after Laurette had met Etienne. He was tall and handsome and older than she was, by about three years. Etienne was the leader of his local group in Paris. Laurette always seemed to fall for the older boys, the ones that seemed so confident, the ones everyone relied on. Perhaps it had something to do with her childhood and the need to find a strong father figure, something lacking in her personal life.

On the first night of the conference, Laurette sat next to Etienne during dinner. She had noticed him immediately. He had golden blond hair and beautiful blue eyes. All the young ladies seemed to want to be close to him. When he'd smiled and asked Laurette her name, she had blushed at the sound of his lilting Parisian accent. She blinked shyly and introduced herself, telling him that this was her first time in France. Etienne quickly took her hand and asked if he could be her personal escort. Of course she agreed. He then proceeded to introduce her to many of his friends and the two became inseparable for the rest of the conference. When it was time for Laurette to board the train back to Belgium, Etienne had kissed her softly and said "Au revoir," promising he would write to her.

While the rest of her friends in *Les Faucons Rouges* were merrily chatting about their exciting experiences in Paris, Laurette sat near the back of the train moping and feeling very sorry for herself. She didn't know if she would ever hear from Etienne again. She felt so empty and alone, just as she had found someone to take care of her and give her confidence. Now she had to leave him behind in another country and return to her troubled life in Brussels where she had to work hard, help care for her brothers, and try to avoid the drunken tirades of her father. While Laurette reflected on the misery of her life, a leader of her own group, a very attractive dark-haired Austrian boy with beautiful dark-brown eyes, took a seat next to her and listened as she poured out her broken heart.

"You'll get over him," he comforted.

Laurette looked up at the older boy. "You don't understand," she sighed.

She allowed herself to be distracted from her self-pity for a moment. She turned her thoughts from the longing for Etienne whom she had left at the train station in Paris, to ponder what she knew of the young man who was trying to comfort her now.

"He may be older and more experienced, but I don't believe Alfred's heart has ever been broken like this," she thought to herself.

"He is always so sure of himself," she mused. "He was able to move to Belgium, learn a new language and become a leader and advisor in such a short time. He was even a translator during the retreat in Paris. I don't think he has ever even had time to have a girlfriend."

Laurette reflected back on the time that had passed since she had first noticed the new boy from Austria who had joined their group. It had been maybe just a year. She couldn't remember seeing Alfred with any one girl during that time, except maybe Louise, who tended to hang around him enough to become a bit of a nuisance.

Laurette smiled momentarily as she thought about the first time she had seen Alfred. She knew instantly that he would soon become one of the leaders from the way he quietly commanded respect from the other young people. He was not especially tall or strong-looking; in fact, he had a rather delicate build for a young man in his early twenties. But he was bright and so sincere that people naturally trusted him.

Laurette had begun to have a bit of a crush on him before the trip to Paris. She loved to flirt and 'make eyes' at him. Alfred had the warmest eyes that twinkled when he smiled, as they did now while he listened to Laurette's woeful tale.

"It's funny," she thought to herself, "I have always found Fredo to be a really nice guy, *'sympathique'*," (or *'sympa'* as her girlfriends would say about a really neat guy.) "I might even have wanted to go out with him. But right now I can only dream of Etienne, and Alfred's attempts to comfort me as if I were a child are only making me feel worse. I have no intention of 'getting over' this and as soon as I can afford to, I'm going back to Paris to be with Etienne."

But she didn't go back, and she never heard from Etienne again.

CHAPTER 4

December 1935
Brussels

It was slightly less than four months since the trip to Paris. Laurette was now 15 and she had begun working at a department store in town. She had started out as a clerk in the receiving area logging in packages and pricing them. It wasn't a very interesting place to work and it didn't pay very well. But her family was relying on her, now more than ever, to help support them financially.

Just two weeks earlier, her father had become seriously ill with a duodenal ulcer. After the operation, everyone thought he would recover. Then, unexpectedly, he had taken a turn for the worse and had died very suddenly. Now there was just Laurette and her brother Roger to take care of her mother and young Jacques.

With the death of her father, Laurette's income became more important than ever in supporting the family. Out of compassion after her father's death, Laurette's employer had offered her a position in the stockroom handling shoes so she could make a little more money. Laurette soon found herself stuck in a room with no windows. It was lonely and she was feeling very sorry for herself. Even the thought of meeting her friend Willie after work didn't please her at all. Willie had been waiting for her every day after work for the past two months. But he was so painfully shy, even more so than she was, that together they would ride the trolley all the way home each night without exchanging a single word.

"I can't stand the thought of riding on the trolley in silence next to Willie for one more night," Laurette lamented.

So she grabbed her black sweater, threw it over her black mourning dress, and headed out the door of the stockroom. When she came out onto La Rue Verte as she did every evening, she turned right instead of left and walked to the opposite corner to keep from running into Willie. But this time, someone else was waiting for her. As she paused a moment, lost in her own thoughts, she felt someone looking at her.

"Fredo, what are you doing here?" she asked with genuine surprise.

"Waiting for you!" he replied, as if she should have naturally been expecting him.

ﻌﻌﻌ

So that is how my parents' long relationship began. Soon their friends in Les Faucons Rouges *began to notice that their leader was paying special attention to one of the members. And this is how I imagine the poignant moments of that special day in May, 1936.*

CHAPTER 5

May 1, 1936
Brussels

Les Faucons Rouges started their hike through the woods. Fredo was teaching the group a new song. He had translated the lyrics into French from a German marching song he had learned years before with the *Rote Falken* in Austria. The girls were giggling at the sounds the boys were making. Even the birds and squirrels seemed to want to get in on the chatter. Above them delicately pointed buds were just barely poking through the cold brown branches of winter. Tiny patches of tender new grass were sprinkled along the trails like peach fuzz on the face of an adolescent boy.

The sun had passed its zenith an hour before. Many members of the group began to unbutton their sweaters and jackets, exposing the blue shirts and red kerchiefs which were the signature "uniform" of the Red Falcons.

"J'ai faim. I'm hungry," yelled Henri.

"Moi aussi. Me too," chimed several voices and soon they were pulling out bread and cheese and fruits. Some of them plopped to the ground while others scrambled to find a rock to sit on as they ate.

Laurette was both hungry and thirsty. She opened her rucksack and was pleased to find the large apple she had packed. She took a large crunchy bite. The juice was sweet and thirst-quenching. Laurette watched as some of her friends drank from the water fountain, thinking, "Boy am I glad this group doesn't allow us to drink alcohol." Through her father, Laurette had seen the damage that too much whiskey and wine could cause. Smoking was forbidden in *Les Faucons Rouges* as well, and she was glad of that. Although she knew many people, adults especially, who were rarely without a cigarette or pipe in their mouths, smoking held no allure for Laurette.

Suddenly Laurette felt someone taking her by the arm. It was Alfred. She wondered momentarily why he was trying to move on when most of the others were still eating. Laurette, in fact, was still nibbling on a piece of fresh crusty bread from her rucksack.

"Let's go," he said. "I want to show you something. We'll be back before the others even notice we're gone."

Laurette glanced around as she stood up. Nearly everyone was still eating and talking. A few had stretched out on the ground.

"Where are we going?" she asked.

"You'll see," Fredo replied.

Typical. He was always a little mysterious. And even though they had been "going together" for several months, he rarely held Laurette's hand. She had noticed, however, that during the ceremonial greeting at the beginning and end of each meeting of *Les Faucons Rouges* he would always wait to shake her hand last so he could hold it just a bit longer than anyone else's. It was a small gesture that most people wouldn't notice, but it meant a lot to Laurette.

Even now, while he stood very close, he touched her arm only slightly as they walked. Soon they were out of sight of the rest of the group, although they could still hear the voices in the distance. As they rounded a bend in the trail, they came to a small clearing that was covered with *muguet de bois*–lilies of the valley. Their sweet fragrance wafted through the spring air.

"Mmm," Laurette sighed, "how beautiful!"

Alfred leaned over and picked one of the prettiest flowers with a profusion of the fragrant little white bells. He presented the flower to Laurette with a dramatic flair and then kissed her right on the mouth. Her heart raced! He had finally kissed her! She was almost giddy with delight and shock. It was so unexpected, and so romantic. She would always remember her first kiss from Fredo came on the first of May.

"Come on," he said, "We'd better return to the group. They'll be ready to continue our hike by now."

Laurette's eyes were still closed. She wanted to savor that moment. She knew she would replay it again and again.

"Okay" she replied reluctantly as he took her hand–yes, he held her hand as they hurried to rejoin their friends.

Laurette wondered if anyone else noticed the extra spring in her step as she danced at the *Manifestation*, the May Day Celebration, that evening. The group was partying at *La Maison du Peuple*, a gathering place where they often met to sing and dance in the back room called the "*tabagie*." Laurette had a beautiful voice and she loved to sing. And on this special occasion, more special than any other she'd yet experienced, she sang long into the night.

Linda Linton

❦❦❦

We were beginning to get a picture of what my parents' life was like when they first began to go together. As they continued their story, we learned of the friendships and associations they were developing. Some of those contacts were very prominent people in the Belgian Government. Yet, the couple was still quite young. I could just envision my mother as a teenager, gossiping with her girlfriend.

CHAPTER 6

June 1938
A Café in Brussels

Laurette set down her cup of tea and smiled at her friend, Zuzu. They hadn't had a chance to catch up on each other's lives for several months and many things had happened.

"So, Laurette, how's work?" her friend asked.

"I'm so glad to be working in the Social Service office now," she sighed. "It is certainly better than the time I spent working for you in that depressing windowless stockroom full of shoes!"

They both laughed at the memory of that poor little girl working long hours in a stuffy room. The friendship they'd developed when Zuzu was Laurette's supervisor was the only thing Laurette enjoyed about that job.

When she had finally left the department store, after less than a year, Laurette worked for several months as an assistant in the local pharmacy, filling pill bottles. Then, through a contact of Alfred's at the social services organization called *"La Femme Prévoyante,"* Laurette had been offered a job doing some filing for the social services group. She had even been encouraged by Madame Maquinet, the same contact who had gotten her the job, to apply for a scholarship at a school called *L'École Ouvrière* in their Social Work program. Although she wasn't initially anxious to go back to school, Laurette knew this school had an excellent program in social work. It was an area of study that interested her and would open significant opportunities to find work when her studies were completed. A scholarship would provide her with room and board while she completed her studies.

"Madame Maquinet has been terrific," Laurette told Zuzu. "She not only got me this filing job, she is even trying to arrange a scholarship for me to attend *L'École Ouvrière*."

"Super!" exclaimed Zuzu, "I've heard about Madame Maquinet and the marvelous

things she's been doing with *La Femme Prévoyante*. Does this mean you will become a social worker?"

"Yes, exactly, but it will require lots of work. I will have two years of theory, a year of work-internship, and then I'll have to write a thesis to get my license!"

"No problem, Laurette, you were always *formidable* when it came to studying."

Laurette shrugged modestly, then continued animatedly to talk about the school:

"Did you know that Claire Barril is a professor at *L'École*?"

"You mean the Commissioner of Ixelles?" Zuzu's eyes grew larger with great interest. Ixelles was the section of Brussels where Laurette lived and it was exciting to get to know someone in the local government on a more personal level.

"Precisely. She is also the Vice-Mayor. I have met her only a few times, but I think Fredo knows her pretty well."

"Nice connection." Zuzu was a bit envious of her friend, "She's plugged in to all the high authorities in the Belgian Government."

"Yes, that is true," Laurette replied. "Through his leadership in *Les Faucons Rouges*, Alfred has become quite friendly with a number of important people in the local government. He has often spoken with our National Assemblywoman, Isabelle Bloom. And, one of the members of Parliament, Jean Husdens, is a very close friend. They play chess together all the time!"

"Impressive! So, how is old Fredo, anyway? You two have been seeing a lot of each other lately, *n'est-ce pas*?"

Laurette's eyes glazed over. "Alfred is very special. But he worries me sometimes. He seems to have so many talents and he is great with *Les Faucons Rouges*. But he doesn't seem to have much luck keeping a job."

"What do you mean?"

"Well, his papa had set him up at the insurance company. But he seemed to be more interested in the photography he does with his German friend, Walter, on the weekends. He got involved with making some 8-mm movies, too. He did one about the opening of a nursing home for the insurance company. I never saw that one. But he did show me his award-winner called H-2-O"

"Award-winner?" Zuzu was a bit skeptical.

"Yes. He won a prize from the Belgian government!"

"Good for him!"

"He left the insurance company and tried his luck at advertising with a cousin of his, but that didn't work out. Now he is selling office supplies for Monsieur Robinson on a commission-only basis.

"Sounds a little tenuous."

"It is," Laurette responded, appearing quite concerned.

Falcons' Flight

"Well, I wouldn't worry, Laurette," her friend comforted her, "He's still young and handsome with ambition and apparently some talent, *non*?"

"I suppose you're right." But Laurette didn't sound convinced.

ôôôô

As we continued to listen to my parents describe their life in Belgium more than fifty years ago, I looked around the hotel room at my niece and nephews. I wondered how their young minds were reacting to this story about their grandparents, especially when my Dad broke the news from the Commissioner....

CHAPTER 7

June 10, 1938
City Hall, Brussels

Fredo turned pale and nearly passed out. He stared at Madame Claire Barril in disbelief. The Vice-Mayor and Commissioner of the municipality of Ixelles had been kind enough to see him on short notice. Alfred knew he was facing a dilemma. He was holding an official notice stating that because he was a non-national and had no steady job, his work permit would not be renewed and he would have to leave Belgium immediately. He had come to Madame Barril for advice. Alfred had worked with her many times in the past and valued her opinion as a friend. But he couldn't quite believe that what she was recommending was truly his only option.

"You must be mistaken. There has to be some other choice."

"Alfred," she said, shaking his deportation notice, "you *must* do as I've suggested if you want to stay in Belgium. There is no other way. Unless you wish to…"

"I couldn't possibly go back to Austria now," he said, completing her thought.

Of course she understood. It would surely be dangerous for him to return to Vienna now. Hitler had taken power and Nazi oppression, especially of Jews, was spreading through Austria.

"Okay then," Madame Barril said suddenly, "let's call Paul Henri Spaak and see what he has to say."

To Alfred's surprise, she immediately lifted her telephone receiver and called the Foreign Minister. Together they persuaded Alfred to make a decision about staying in Belgium. Finally, he agreed and thanked the Commissioner for her time and trouble.

"Merci, Madame," he said softly as he took the letter from her hand and turned toward the door.

"You don't have much time to decide, Alfred," she called after him.

Falcons' Flight

"I understand, *Madame*," he said politely as he closed the door to her chamber.

Outside in the air he felt only slightly revived. His arms were heavy. He took in a deep breath. Suddenly he felt old. The world around him was closing in. Things weren't simple any longer. There was a great deal of political unrest and no one knew where it would lead. But one thing was certain: Alfred could not allow his status as an unemployed alien to force him to return to the potential dangers in Austria.

In that moment, Alfred made a decision that would change his life forever.

Alfred's hand was trembling as he reached up to press the doorbell outside Laurette's apartment building.

"*Bonjour*, Alfred." Laurette's mother opened the door for him to enter.

"*Merci*, Madame Deprince," he said, his pale face gazing blankly at his shoes as he stepped inside.

She peered at him with a skeptical squint. He was clearly not well. His pallor made his face look drawn and he was visibly shaking.

"*Salut*, Fredo," Laurette greeted him cheerfully as she bounded into the room. She stopped in her tracks when she saw his face.

"Alfred, what is it?"

He looked at her, then at her mother, then back at Laurette.

"Sit down, Alfred," insisted Laurette's mother.

They all sat gingerly, literally on the edge of their seats.

"We have to get married," he blurted without warning.

"What!!" Laurette and her mother gasped simultaneously.

"Yes. It's the only way I can stay in Belgium. I must marry a Belgian girl."

Madame DePrince looked with disapproval at her 17-year-old daughter sitting next to this trembling young Austrian boy with no steady job. She wanted to respond instantly with the instinct of a protective mother and say "no, this is impossible." Instead, with great restraint and the wisdom of a simple woman who has lived a hard life, she began to ask the important questions. Where would they live? How would they make a living? How much would Laurette continue to contribute to her family's income?

They began to find some reason in this madness. And by the end of the evening, it was all settled. The wedding was set for June 18th.

CHAPTER 8

June 18, 1938
City Hall, Brussels

Alfred had taken care of all the details. City Hall was a suitable place for the wedding since Alfred was a non-practicing Jew and Laurette, raised Catholic, stopped going to church at age 13. Claire Barril, both their friend and Vice-Mayor of the municipality of Ixelles, would perform the ceremony.

After the ceremony there would be a very small reception at the Blue Danube Café. Alfred had arranged for a typically Viennese dinner with Wienerschnitzel and wine.

The small wedding party gathered nervously in the great hall outside the Vice-Mayor's chambers. There were several wedding ceremonies scheduled ahead of theirs and they were forced to wait for much of the afternoon. The minutes ticked by very slowly. Laurette and her maid of honor, Louisette, fussed over her hair and hat as Laurette's mother and two brothers looked on. Jean, the best man, tried to keep the groom distracted by telling silly jokes as they paced across the hall. Alfred began to think of his family–his parents, his two sisters, and his brother. It would have been wonderful if they had been there to support him and help celebrate. But he was unable to contact them for fear of exposing them or himself to investigation by the Nazis. He didn't dare risk placing his family in danger.

One by one the groups of newlywed couples and their families came through the doorway smiling and congratulating one another. Outside the bells from the church at the end of the street were chiming. Laurette stopped for a moment to listen. Even though her family had never been very religious, she found comfort in the clanging sound of the great bells in the steeple of the Catholic Church, an especially appropriate sound today.

"*Liebermann-Deprince mariage,*" someone announced. Laurette's heart began to race. Alfred grew a bit pale again.

Wedding Portrait, Alfred and Laurette Liebermann, June 18, 1938

"This is it!" he thought to himself.

The ceremony was short and sweet. They said their vows. Rings were exchanged. All the appropriate documents were signed and witnessed. Then, unexpectedly, Madame Barril stepped down from her high desk and came over to kiss the bride and groom.

"Felicitations et bonne chance! Congratulations and good luck," she said as she hugged the happy young couple.

Laurette and Alfred were pleased that Claire Barril had been able to conduct the ceremony. The guests, meanwhile, were amazed that so prominent a person would step down from her desk to greet their wedding party.

At the restaurant, the guests were enjoying their Wienerschnitzel and the happy chatter so much they didn't pay much attention to the wine Alfred had selected. It was Tokay, a Hungarian wine and the only one he knew by name. As an inexperienced drinker, he had no idea that Tokay was a sweet, heavy dessert wine.

When the festivities were over, the party agreed to meet at Laurette's mother's house where several additional family members were gathered to congratulate the newlyweds. Laurette's head was swimming with all the excitement…and the wine. She and her new husband ran to catch the trolley back to her former home. That was a strange new thought--her former home.

As the trolley rumbled down the streets of Brussels, Laurette tried to focus. Was she really married? At age 17? What would happen to them now? How would her family get along without her? She felt dizzy. The last few hours blurred together–the preparations, the ceremony, that huge Wienerschnitzel that hung over the edge of her plate, the noise, the wine, oh the wine.

Suddenly Laurette realized she was going to be sick and there was nothing she could do. She couldn't hold out any longer. She threw up all the wedding food and drink right there on the trolley!

Fredo tried to comfort her as the trolley rumbled on toward his mother-in-law's home.

When they arrived, Laurette changed her clothes, greeted the new guests, and went on with the celebration.

xxx

This was the first time my parents had ever revealed to us any details about their wedding, and what details they were! It seemed especially remarkable, and appropriate, to be hearing this story for the first time as we celebrated their 50th wedding anniversary! And if we thought the circumstances of the wedding were unique, we were about to discover that their first weeks of married life were unusual as well.

xxx

Alfred and Laurette Liebermann spent their honeymoon back-packing in the mountains, hiking along a river in eastern Belgium. The trip was lovely, but oh so brief. They were gone only for a weekend, then returned to the mansard room that Alfred had been renting from a family just outside of Brussels. The room wasn't much, but it was cozy.

One reason for their short honeymoon trip was that Laurette had volunteered as a camp aide and was responsible for taking a group of children to the seashore for three weeks. What a way to start a new life together with a ready-made family of 35 children!

For the most part, the youngsters were well behaved. They ranged in age from nine to thirteen, both boys and girls. Alfred brought his guitar along and taught them some of his favorite songs. Laurette always loved to sing along. It made the time pass much more quickly.

This could have been a romantic time for the newlyweds to walk hand in hand along the sandy beach looking at the beautiful sea. But instead, Laurette was far too busy treating the cuts and scrapes and itchy rashes of the children to enjoy the scenery or indulge in young romance. One little girl came down with impetigo and every morning Laurette had to clean the child's wounds. What an unpleasant reminder that this was not a honeymoon!

Thank goodness Laurette had learned so many things about simple medical care from her mother as she was growing up. Juliette was no scholar, having finished school only through the fourth grade. But she was wise and had surprisingly practical answers to the many challenges of caring for children when they are sick or injured. Some of her methods and treatments, perhaps, might have been called "witches brews." But most of her "home remedies," from mustard plasters and poultices to herbal teas, had been passed down through generations and the truth is, many of them really worked. And these remedies came in handy while Laurette was fulfilling her role as leader and nurse on this trip.

Meanwhile, Alfred spent much of the time photographing the children–in groups and individually–as they played in the sand and water. He had become quite adept with his Leica camera. As he completed each roll of film, he would send it back to Brussels to Walter, a German refugee Alfred had befriended and with whom he had done some photography work in the past. Walter specialized in photography with Leica equipment, so the photos were as professionally developed as they were skillfully shot.

The children went crazy over the 8 x 10 pictures. Their parents were so impressed with the quality of the photographs that they ordered them on the spot. So, before he knew it, Alfred had started a photography business.

෨෨෨

When I think back through my own childhood, I remember Daddy always took great photographs. I even recall seeing photographic developing equipment in our basement in Philadelphia. I also remember how devastated he was when our car was broken into in New York City and his Leica was stolen. I don't ever recall him being so upset about any possessions as he was about the loss of that camera. Now I understand why.

As my father continued to describe their first year of marriage, the next part of the story came as quite a shock...

CHAPTER 9

November 1938
Brussels

It was a brisk day in early November when Alfred received an urgent telegram from his mother in Vienna:

"Your father has been taken to a German labor camp in upper Bavaria, northeast of Munich. STOP. Mother."

Alfred was stunned. He and Laurette had been hearing rumors about the arrest of some prominent individuals in Vienna, especially those of Jewish background. But they never expected to hear that Alfred's father was taken to Dachau to work as a common laborer!

Alfred had to act quickly. He knew that his brother and two sisters had already fled the dangers in Austria and found passage, through Cuba, to the United States. Papers for their travels had been arranged through a relative of John Hirschfeld, who had married Alfred's sister, Erna. Alfred contacted John and learned that he had already cabled the paperwork to Vienna to Alfred's mother for her to obtain two Cuban visas for herself and Alfred's father. But they were in need of a transit visa through Belgium in order to leave Austria.

Alfred set to work using all of his connections with influential officials of the Belgian government. There were meetings and calls to the Belgian Foreign Minister and the Chief of *Sûreté Publique*, (the local police). Then came hours and days of desperate waiting. Finally Alfred succeeded in having the order for the issuance of the visas transmitted by telegram to the Belgian Embassy in Vienna.

The receipt of the transit visas enabled his mother and several of his father's loyal friends to pay off the authorities and somehow they managed to have Norbert released from the camp.

Falcons' Flight

❧❧❧

Apparently they were able to free my grandfather just in the nick of time. He was one of a very few prisoners to be liberated from Dachau before it became one of the notorious death camps!

❧❧❧

As soon as Norbert Liebermann arrived home in Vienna, he and Leontine immediately arranged to leave the country. They spent ten days with Alfred and his new wife in Brussels, then departed from Antwerp, Belgium, for Cuba. About a month later, Alfred and Laurette received word that his parents had arrived safely in America and together with Alfred's brother, Otto, were living in Philadelphia.

❧❧❧

Now everyone in my father's immediate family had successfully fled Austria. His parents and siblings were starting over in America, far from Nazi persecution. Meanwhile, my parents were finally managing to establish their life in Brussels where they also thought they would be safe.

Linda Linton

CHAPTER 10

May 1, 1940
Brussels

It was nearly two years after they had been married when Alfred and Laurette Liebermann were finally able to afford to rent an apartment of their own. It was located on the top floor of a five-story building in downtown Brussels, and they moved in on May 1, 1940. Alfred was working full time with Walter at the photography studio, and Laurette was well into her studies in preparation for her degree in social work. Things were finally beginning to feel secure in their personal lives.

They were still keeping contact with their friends from *Les Faucons Rouges* and would often get together in the evenings to listen to the radio and discuss politics. There was much talk about the activities of the German Nazi party and wild speculation as to what Adolf Hitler might try to do next. He had already marched triumphantly through Vienna, on Alfred's 23rd birthday, of all days, two years before on March 14, 1938.

[Historical Note: In this bold move, Hitler had proclaimed Austria reunified with Germany. Following the Anschluss, it became evident that this man was determined to expand his realm. Despite promises to world leaders at the Munich Conference in September 1938 to end his expansion with cession of the Sudetenland, Hitler proceeded to make plans to take over Czechoslovakia. And on March 16, 1939, just one year after the Anschluss in Austria, the "German Protectorate of Bohemia and Moravia" was established. Only a few days later, Hitler began making demands on Poland, attempting to incorporate Danzig into Germany. The demands were rejected, with the British and French pledging guarantees for territorial integrity of Poland in late March. By April, 1939, Hitler canceled the Non-aggression Pact with Poland, and the Anglo-German Naval Agreement. He then went on to sign a Non-aggression Pact with the Soviet Union in August and subsequently attacked Poland on September 1st. Mussolini proclaimed Italy a "non-belligerent" power. But when the demands of Britain and France for withdrawal of German forces from Poland were rejected, war was declared on September 3, 1939.

The Red Army invaded Eastern Poland on September 17th, which led to the German-Soviet Border and

Falcons' Flight

Friendship Treaty, signed on September 28th. In November, 1939 the Soviet Union attacked Finland leading to the expulsion of the USSR from the League of Nations in December. By March, 1940, the Peace of Moscow was concluded in order to avert conflict with the Western Nations. Meanwhile, Germany had occupied Denmark and Norway in April, 1940.]

Rumors abounded that Hitler was planning to invade Britain. There was talk that he was even threatening to bring troops into Holland and Belgium as well. But no one wanted to believe that the war would hit so close to home.

May 10, 1940, 5:30 A.M.
Brussels

KABOOM!

A thunderous crash woke Alfred and Laurette with a jolt. Flashes of light shot across the sky. It was like a split-second explosion of a violent thunderstorm on the hottest day in August. But it was only early May. Laurette felt a tingling in her nostrils and the choking smell of something burning. Smoke wafted past her in its rush to fill the room. Her eyes began to sting. She rubbed them fiercely in an attempt to rid herself of the nightmare that had awakened her from a deep sleep.

"What's going on?" Laurette asked as she and Alfred scrambled to the window. They couldn't believe what they were witnessing. Planes flew overhead and sirens began to scream. It was clear this was no thunderstorm.

At first Laurette thought it might be the Belgian warplanes that sometimes flew overhead during maneuvers, but that would have been unusual at this time of the morning. As she was trying to assimilate what was happening around her, Laurette heard Alfred whisper in a tone of fear she had rarely heard him use:

"It's the Germans." They both stared in disbelief, mesmerized by the sounds and sights.

"An air raid? Oh please, no!" Laurette said.

"I think one of the bombs landed on our roof!"

"What shall we do?!"

"Since it hasn't exploded, it must be a dud—or maybe an incendiary bomb." Alfred was yelling now. The drone of the German warplanes was deafening.

"We can't go outside," he said. "This building is the best protection we have. The sandbags on the roof should keep us safe as long as we don't get a direct hit with an explosive bomb. Then nothing could help us anyway."

They both began to shiver with shock. This was a nightmare come true. The roar of the airplanes was fading slightly but the sirens screamed on and on. Laurette tried to shake the paralyzing feeling of helplessness. Her thoughts were jumbled.

"I hope my mother and my brothers are okay. Oh, why don't the Germans leave us alone? What have we done to deserve this?"

After what seemed like an eternity, the sirens finally began to subside and the airplanes were sounding more and more distant. The early morning was beginning to dawn with an eerie brown light. There was none of the usual morning clatter from the vendors in the market square. You couldn't hear the junk man collecting bottles calling *"des bouteilles"* as he did every other morning. The trucks that usually delivered flowers and milk and produce to the local market were nowhere in sight. No cats could be heard fighting in the alleyway.

The grinding propeller sounds of the warplanes slowly died away. In their place was another unfamiliar sound, off in the distance. In a bizarre way, it reminded Laurette of an approaching parade. Not like music, really, more like a carnival barker. The voice sounded Belgian and the language was French, but the manner was gruff and stilted. As the voice grew nearer, Alfred picked up some of the words.

"...Foreigners...non-Belgian nationals...register...police station...immediately!"

"Oh no!" Laurette gasped. They both knew all too well that even though Alfred was now married to a Belgian girl, he was still considered a foreigner.

"What do we do now, Fredo?"

"I guess we go down to the police station!"

CHAPTER 11

May 10, 1940, Afternoon
Brussels

The police station was mobbed. Everyone was talking about the air raid and about the war. Most of the faces were unfamiliar to Laurette and Alfred, and they were all tense with worry. No one knew what to expect. Names were being called over the din of nervous chatter.

"Edlemeyer…Frankel…Goldblum…"

"Frankel!" Laurette suddenly sat very straight. "I went to school with someone by that name. Oh, Alfred, what is going to happen?"

"Don't worry." He tried to comfort her. "I know the Police Chief of the district very well. He will process me quickly and this will all be over in no time."

Laurette wasn't so sure. Even though Alfred had many good connections in the city government, no one knew what to expect or even whom to trust.

"Liebermann…"

"Wait here," Alfred said to his wife. "I won't be long."

Then he kissed her and held her for a brief moment. He seemed so confident while Laurette was shaking.

Alfred walked through the double doors along with dozens of other men.

"Pawlowski…Rabinsky…Rosenfeld…Schmidt…"

Alfred's friend Joseph Schmidt walked by and squeezed Laurette's hand. Laurette smiled at the young man they had always called Schmidt.

"Don't worry, *mon amie*," he said to Laurette, "Everything will be all right. I'll keep an eye on Fredo and make sure he doesn't get into any trouble. We'll be back out in time for dinner, you'll see." Then Laurette watched her husband's friend filing behind the others.

There was something in his tone that seemed to say he wasn't so sure they would be back at all.

Laurette sat and stared at the double doors. The stream of men seemed to go on forever. Laurette tried to sound optimistic as she made idle conversation with the other wives, girlfriends, mothers, and children.

"This is only a formality," said one woman. "They must follow the rules carefully to avoid having to make any explanations. This morning's air raid was only a warning."

"I think the war is nearly over already," said one young girl. "Hitler is losing his influence in Germany. The French want nothing to do with him. He won't be in power much longer. Then things will go back to the way they were."

Laurette wasn't so sure she believed anything these people were saying. She glanced around the room. Some of the children were playing games on the floor. Several older women were sitting together in a circle staring blankly at the few small windows near the ceiling. Their knitting needles were clicking madly. Many were reading the newspaper. A few had even brought a book to read.

Laurette wished she had brought some of her needlepoint. It was frustrating to sit for so many hours, worried about what was going to happen to Alfred, with nothing to keep her nervous hands busy. Nearly five hours had passed since Alfred had gone in to register. And not one of the people who had gone in through the double doors had come back through them. Nor had any official come out to report on what was going on.

Laurette began to hear rumors that those who had gone through the doors to register would be kept overnight.

"I must run home and pack a rucksack for Alfred," she began planning as she quickly said goodbye to those who were waiting around her.

Laurette had no idea what was to happen, but if she could at least get a change of clothes to her husband, he might feel a little bit more comfortable through this seemingly interminable waiting period. And she, at least, could temporarily quell this awful feeling of helplessness by doing *something*.

"Let's see, underwear, a fresh shirt, socks, what else?" Laurette fumbled through drawers in a daze.

"I know, I should pack him something to eat. I have no idea if they have fed anyone." She ran to the kitchen and grabbed some cheese and bread, a bunch of grapes, and an apple.

Then Laurette hurried out the door and ran back down the five flights of stairs. Her heart was pounding with fear and excitement. She didn't even think to stop to take the elevator. It wouldn't have mattered anyway because Alfred had the key in his pocket and Laurette would have been unable to use the elevator without that key.

Winded and perspiring, Laurette pushed passed the crowd that was still awaiting the return of their loved ones at the police station. She approached a guard by the door.

"My husband was here to register early this morning and he is still inside. I have brought him something to eat. Could you please see that he gets this? His name is Alfred Liebermann."

The guard looked at Laurette with slight amusement. She was so young, too young to be married, he thought. She was quite attractive, though obviously distraught.

"*Oui, Madame*," he said taking the rucksack from her. "Monsieur Liebermann. I will see that he gets this."

The guard disappeared behind the door, momentarily avoiding many of the others who were pleading for information about their family members.

Several more hours crept by. Laurette had begun to doze in the late afternoon sunlight that was piercing through the small window by the benches where she and the others had been waiting.

"May I have your attention please." It was the guard who had taken the rucksack. "Those people who have gone in to register today will be detained here until tomorrow. Anyone awaiting a relative or friend is encouraged to leave and return in the morning."

Laurette's heart sank. She slowly filed out behind the others feeling dejected and exhausted. She could hear several of the others speculating on how long it would be before these people would be released.

"Certainly it will all be over by morning," said one older woman.

"Mommy, where have they taken Papa?" cried a little girl with long brown hair and a small pink bow.

"He is going to be away for a while," her mother said, then tried to comfort the child. "We're going to go home and pack him a nice suitcase with all his favorite things, okay, little one?"

Laurette began to think about the rucksack she had given to the guard. There was barely enough in there for one day. If the police were planning to hold these people until things quieted down, it could be days, maybe even weeks.

As she began to climb the five flights of stairs to her apartment, Laurette felt terribly alone.

Early the next morning, Laurette carried a large suitcase filled with whatever she could fit of Alfred's clothes, toiletries, and food down the five flights and over to the police station. Thirty or forty others were already there. Soon the station would once again be jammed with anxious faces. Rumors were flying now that the "prisoners," as many called them, were taken to the local garrison across from the railroad station. For the first time, Laurette began to think about the work camps like the one from which they had rescued Alfred's father. She began to visualize the wretched conditions. The fleas and the lice. The cramped quarters with little or no food. The dysentery and the lack of toilet facilities.

"Dear God," she whispered, "Please don't let them send him to one of those camps in Poland or Germany."

The hours crawled by even more slowly than they had the day before. Laurette read a little, but had trouble concentrating. She had some sewing with her, but soon finished whatever projects she had brought.

Finally, her stomach started to growl. She hadn't eaten for nearly ten hours. She was beginning to feel faint from lack of food and little sleep.

"Come on Laurette, you've got to eat something."

One of Laurette's friends, Monique, had been walking past the police station with her husband and had stopped in when they saw so many familiar faces.

"Why don't you come home with us and have some supper?" Monique pleaded. "I'm sure nothing critical will take place while we are gone. You'll feel much better after a meal."

Laurette was too tired to argue. And the thought of eating actually began to revive her.

" A quick bite and we'll come right back?"

"Absolutely," Monique assured her.

Laurette was only gone for an hour. All kinds of rumors were spreading now of the whereabouts of all the people who had "registered," and the moment she walked back in the door of the police station, she could sense something had just happened. In the confusion and noise, Laurette was able to learn that the group had been spotted at the garrison, as some had feared. The prisoners were preparing to board a train and if their loved ones hurried, they could pass the suitcases to their husbands and sons over the fence outside the garrison as they filed by.

Laurette quickly followed the crowd onto the trolley and over to the garrison. As she stepped down from the trolley, she could see the men lined up behind the fence. She caught a glimpse of a small man with a blue rucksack.

"Alfred!" she yelled. People turned around to look. She thought he might have heard her, but she wasn't sure. He seemed to be close to the gate, but no one was moving. Some of the men, including Joseph Schmidt, did have a suitcase. It was evident that their wives had been able to pass them over the fence. But it was too late for Laurette to get the suitcase to Alfred. She could just see his small frame as a freight train roared in and stopped right in front of the group, blocking her view completely. It was impossible to reach him.

The row of cattle cars looked endless.

"Cattle cars," Laurette gasped. "They are going to force all of these people into those horrible boxes! Oh, my God."

The men were herded into the cars and the train slowly pulled out. The engine grunted and spat smoke as it began to gain speed. Car after car went by in a dizzying blur. *Chugga chugga, chugga chugga.* It was already a considerable distance down the track when the engineer blew the long whistle. Laurette had a momentary flashback to another train, the train that had separated her from her first love. How trivial the pain of that first separation now seemed! Now, at age 19, she stared blankly at the huge moving boxes, one of which carried her husband to who-knew-where.

And then there was the ugly, deafening silence.

ভ্তভ্তভ্ত

For years I had read about the cattle cars that were used to transport people during World War II. I had seen documentaries of the brutal conditions, the horrible treatment by the soldiers and the unthinkable destinies of the thousands upon thousands of innocent people, many of them Jews, who suffered through those train rides. I had no idea my father had been one of those people! We were oblivious to the absurd contrast of sitting in a luxury hotel room in Bermuda as we sat transfixed listening to him recount his story. I felt at the same time fascination and disbelief. Imagining my own father under those conditions was nearly impossible for me.

Linda Linton

CHAPTER 12

May 12, 1940
Somewhere outside of Brussels

When the doors of the cattle car had slammed shut, and the train had begun to move out, it took several long moments to adjust to the darkness. There was just a sliver of light piercing through the crack in the door. Once he was able to see enough to get his bearings, Schmidt shoved his suitcase over toward Alfred. He struggled to keep his balance as the train jerked and jostled the passengers who were packed in like the cattle these cars were designed to carry. Some leaned up against the sides of the car. Others were sitting on their suitcases. A few found enough space to sit on the floor. For a car that was known to hold "eight horses or forty people," it was jammed with about 95 people.

The train had chugged and coughed through two days and nights and was slowly making its way to a destination unknown to its passengers. While the conditions were extremely uncomfortable, the Belgian officers remained somewhat considerate of these weary passengers. Then suddenly something changed.

The train had stopped only once in the last 14 hours. When the huge doors slid open, the huddled people inside squinted into the bright sunlight. They remained perfectly still, not knowing what to expect.

The officers were now no longer Belgian. They shouted their abrupt commands with a distinctly French accent:

"*Allez*–everyone out! Those who wish to eat, *à droite*, to the right. Those who need the toilet, *à gauche*, to the left. Quickly!"

The passengers scrambled toward the door and fresh air. They lined up in a military style and were shuffled forward by the French officers. Those on the right were handed a chunk of bread and a cup of water. That was it. Breakfast, lunch, and dinner, and probably tomorrow's breakfast and lunch too, in that one handful of bread.

Those who lined up on the left were hustled to a large hole that had just been dug into the ground in the middle of an open field, where they were able to finally relieve themselves.

"It's amazing how grateful one can feel for something as small and basic as a toilet, albeit a hole in the ground," reflected Alfred as he climbed back into the cattle car behind the others.

The passengers were not permitted to speak to one another, at least not when the officers were watching. When the huge doors were shoved closed, once again it was totally dark inside. No one spoke for a long time. Slowly, as their eyes became accustomed to the darkness, people began to adjust themselves and try to find some comfort in this miserable place.

With a jolt, the train lurched forward and began its familiar *chugga, chugga, chugga.* Alfred could feel something being pressed into his hand. Schmidt had sidled up to him and handed him a small crust of bread.

"After you shared your grapes with me yesterday, I figured it was the least I could do. I noticed you never made it to the line *à droite.*" Alfred was grateful for the morsel of dry bread.

"What about you? Didn't you get to *la toilette*?"

"I can hold out for a while, Fredo. Don't worry about me."

"It seems we've crossed over into France." Alfred whispered to his friend. "I wonder what this means."

"Well, so far as we know, the French are not involved in the war–not yet, at least. But I've read some unsettling things about these people. I'm not sure how safe we will be if they keep us here. You can tell their attitude in general by the way we were treated during that last stop."

"Hopefully this trip will not take much longer. Then when we have arrived at our destination we will know better about the circumstances we are dealing with."

Alfred's thoughts were interrupted when a large figure stumbled toward him and tripped over his rucksack. He was yelling fragments of sentences in German: "My mother won't let me stay in this place…Where are my horses?…Why aren't the children playing here?…I'll kill those bastard French, that's what I'll do…."

Alfred knew him only as Heinz, the German blacksmith. He was such a big, brawny-looking man. And now in the very dim light, Alfred could see this man's eyes rolling slightly as he clenched his fist and cried out again, "I must get to the church…The physician will help us all…My Mama, I need her…."

He collapsed into Alfred's arms and began to sob.

Alfred had been in many situations before where his leadership and even comfort were needed by his companions in various youth organizations. But this was different. Here was a strong, virile blacksmith who had gone mad and was now weeping in his arms. Alfred tried to comfort Heinz as best he could. He rocked the blacksmith like a baby and spoke quietly to him. The others stared in fear and compassion for this man who expressed the outer limits of their own increasingly meager sanity.

Heinz went on sobbing for nearly two hours. Alfred's legs were numb from the weight of this man, but he didn't dare try to move him. At one point, the blacksmith began to choke and gasp for air. He held Alfred's arm in a vise-like grip for a moment. Then Heinz slowly released the hold as a long breath of air whistled through his parted lips. It was his last breath; there was nothing anyone could do. In a way, the others almost envied this man who had found his own peace while they stood in terror of the unknown that awaited them.

In the deadly quiet an eerily familiar sound far off in the distance was getting louder. The whir of propellers and the sound of grinding engines were overpowering the constant *chugga, chugga* of the train. Everyone instinctively stooped down low. Some covered their heads with their rucksacks. No one spoke a word but Alfred could feel the people closest to him trembling. Or was that his own small frame shaking with new fear?

KABOOM!!

The world exploded with light and fire. It felt as if millions of bullets were sizzling by in all directions. Actually, it wasn't bullets at all. A German bomb had hit one of the cars which happened to be hauling gravel, and the tiny stones had become deadly projectiles ricocheting in every direction, penetrating the walls of several of the neighboring railroad cars.

In a split second, extensive destruction took place. People were screaming and moaning. There was blood everywhere. The train rumbled on for what seemed like days as people lay dead and dying inside the crowded cattle cars. Some tore off bits of clothing and made an effort to bandage the wounded. Many lay in stunned silence. The already-foul air became dank with the smell of blood.

Alfred was crawling over to help a wounded man when a jolt sent him lurching forward and the train ground to a halt. Those who were still conscious braced themselves in silence. There were sounds of voices outside and great commotion. The now-familiar banging and creaking of the old doors as they slid open was getting closer as the soldiers approached Alfred's car. All at once the door to his car jerked open and in the nearly blinding light Alfred could discern figures climbing aboard and pushing their way through. Loud voices were barking orders while bodies were being dragged past him.

As his eyes adjusted to the light he could see the officers grabbing the dead and tossing them like rag dolls onto the ground near the tracks. Those who were able to walk unassisted were permitted to use the "toilet" while the officers finished disposing of the bodies.

A few moments later the prisoners were herded back into the cars and once again Alfred was locked with the others in this dark, dank, moving prison.

CHAPTER 13

May 15, 1940
Somewhere in France

Several days had gone by. It was very difficult to tell just how much time had passed. The train had stopped only twice since the bombing, just to clear out the dead.

Finally the doors opened again and everyone was forced to get out and walk. Alfred had thought they were getting in line for a morsel of food. His stomach began to grumble in anticipation.

"*Allez, allez vite*! Keep moving, quickly!" The French soldiers were pushing the weary travelers roughly.

It was becoming evident that this was not a routine stop for food or use of the "toilet." They were instead being forced to march a considerable distance. As the refugees marched on, the train slipped out of sight completely. That hungry gurgle in Alfred's stomach turned to one huge silent knot. What had started out as a refreshing hike and a chance to get the circulation moving again had become a terrifying march to an unknown destination. Was this IT? Were they going to a death camp? Or an execution squad?

Alfred noticed some commotion up ahead. Someone up the line stumbled and fell. A soldier came over and kicked him.

"Get up. Stand up, I said!" He kicked the fallen man twice more.

Schmidt was incensed.

"Leave him alone!" he yelled as he threw himself down to protect his fellow refugee.

"Get up, both of you!" insisted the French soldier as he swung the butt of his gun, hitting Schmidt on the side of his head.

At that moment, while Schmidt's head was reeling with pain and confusion, another officer shouted from the other side of the line and everyone came to a halt in front of an old farmhouse with a huge barn.

Falcons' Flight

"All of you, inside!" were the instructions. "You will be staying here for the night".

The soldier glared at Schmidt "Watch yourself, "he said, "or next time I'll use the other end of the gun." And he turned away in a huff.

Once they were inside the barn, Alfred helped Schmidt settle onto the straw. "Are you all right?"

"My head is pounding, Fredo."

"Here, I have something for that pain, if you can take it without water."

Alfred reached into his pocket and pulled out a small packet with two aspirin tablets.

Schmidt regarded his friend with gratitude. Remembering several occasions during their hikes together with the Red Falcons when Alfred would show up with a penknife or a handkerchief at just the right moment, he remarked:

"Somehow, Fredo, you always manage to come prepared for just about anything, don't you!"

"I'm afraid I wasn't quite prepared for this," sighed Alfred as he looked around at all the exhausted, starving people who had been jammed into the barn with them. He handed the pills to his friend who chewed and swallowed them with a grimace.

"Not too tasty, but I am very glad you had them in your pocket, Fredo. Otherwise, I'm not sure what I would have done."

In minutes, Schmidt had drifted off to sleep leaving Alfred staring numbly at the dozens of people lying nearly on top of one other in the hayloft above him.

"Somehow I will survive this," he promised himself as he too faded into a fitful slumber.

Several hours passed. Without warning the barn door swooshed open and a brigade of soldiers entered. This time, a young German officer led the French soldiers as they marched in formation. In his startled, slightly dazed state, Alfred found this little parade almost amusing, as if they had just stepped from the stage of a comic opera. The leader of the parade was a very young Nazi officer, who couldn't have been more than 18 years old.

"*Attention!*" he demanded. The weary refugees stumbled to their feet and stood wide-eyed and as straight as their tired bodies could manage. The whole scene struck Alfred as ridiculous as the soldiers strutted by to inspect their ragged "troops." Alfred just couldn't help the tiny smile that crept across his face.

Suddenly the German officer stopped dead in front of Alfred and pulled his gun. He held the gun right next to Alfred's temple. Instantly the smile left Alfred's face as he froze solid. No one in the room dared to move. The seconds ticked by. Alfred was sure he was going to feel the sting of a bullet splitting his head open.

Then, by some quirk of fate, the young Nazi decided to lower his gun and move on. In that instant, Alfred silently swore never to smile again unless he was sure he was completely alone.

[Historical Note: Alfred's incident with the young Nazi officer indicated that, although France had not yet been formally invaded by the Nazis, German soldiers had already entered the country and started to influence military activities.]

Moments later the refugees were all out in the early morning sunshine, marching in line once again without knowing where they were headed. They walked for many miles through several small French towns. As they trod wearily past the residents of one of the towns, the locals began to spit at them and call them spies and traitors. A few even threw stones.

After the exhausting and humiliating trek through the French countryside, the refugees found themselves at a railroad station where they were forced to stand at attention for what seemed to be an hour or more. They had had nothing to eat or drink since they left the barn several hours earlier. Finally the freight train pulled into the station. One-by-one the refugees were herded back into several cattle cars which again became the moving prison carrying them on a blind journey.

Many hours passed with no food or water and people were beginning to cough and become very weak from thirst. It had begun to rain. The constant pounding of the rain on the roof of the cattle car was mesmerizing to Alfred. In his dazed condition, Alfred thought he saw a tall man lean over and pull something from inside his boot.

Slowly the man began to scrape and turn the object against the ceiling of the car. In the dim light, Alfred could see that he had smuggled in a penknife and was slowly drilling a hole in the ceiling. He scraped and dug for a very long time. No one seemed to pay much attention.

After about an hour, water began to drip from the hole he had made in the ceiling. Cool refreshing rainwater was seeping into the cattle car. People began to clamor toward the hole in the roof. They brought empty cans, bottle tops, rolled paper or just their cupped hands, desperate for a few drops of rainwater. Some pushed at each other, trying to force their way closer to the precious drops. But amazingly, each man managed to get a share.

As Alfred sat down with his handmade paper cup of rainwater, he closed his eyes and drank gratefully. For the first time in several days, he allowed himself to think about Laurette. She would never believe what the past days had been like for him. Better that she didn't know what was happening to her husband, he thought. As he wondered if he would ever see her again, he tried to imagine what she was doing and how she was getting along. Had the Germans occupied Belgium after the bombing? He didn't know for sure, but there was a strong possibility that life in Brussels, as he remembered it, had changed dramatically.

≈≈≈

Everyone in the hotel room in Bermuda was transfixed. It was nearly midnight but none of us wanted to leave. We could hardly believe what we had just heard my parents describe. Imagine Dad being taken away from Brussels in a cattle car jammed full of people with no idea where he would end up. And Mom, at the tender age of 19 and already married for two years, was left behind to worry and wonder where he was going and whether she would ever see him again. We knew it was time to put the children to bed, so we would have to wait until tomorrow to hear the next part of the story....

When we reconvened the next evening, my mother began to tell us her part of the story after Dad was shipped out of Belgium. It was so difficult to envision my own mother at such a young age, all alone during wartime, wondering if she would ever see her husband again....

CHAPTER 14

June 1940
Brussels

Laurette had been dragging herself through the past four weeks in a daze. Without the key to the elevator, which Alfred had in his pocket on the day he was taken away, Laurette had to hike up the five flights of stairs every day. She had no idea where her husband was, none. There had been rumors. Many rumors, but no news. The police simply said that "the non-nationals had been taken away for safe keeping." She had seen the cattle cars as the train pulled away from the station. She knew the officials had squeezed hundreds of people into those cars and the conditions had to have been terrible. But she had no idea where that train had gone. Was it really going to France for "safe keeping," as the officers had told her, or was it a trick? Had they actually been sent to the war front to fight? Or to work camps in Poland or Austria? There had been horrifying stories circulating about so-called "death camps" where hundreds of Jews were being killed or left to die of exposure, disease, and starvation.

Laurette shuddered. She was thinking of one report she'd heard from a friend with a shortwave radio. It happened only a day or two after Alfred's train had pulled out. The report said that German warplanes had bombed a train, somewhere in France. Many people were supposed to have been killed.

Suddenly, as if her mind were imagining the scenes so vividly as to conjure up sound effects, Laurette could hear the sound of approaching airplanes and then the blare of the air-raid sirens. Instinctively now, she reached for her jacket and started back down the stairs toward the air-raid shelter in the cellar that she had come to know so well. Nearly every day, sometimes twice in the same day, she would have to run from the fifth floor down to the shelter in the basement. There she would huddle together with the crying children and the old people and the wretched smells and the trembling, frightened neighbors.

"Today," she promised herself, "when the 'all clear' signal is sounded, I'm getting out of our apartment. I can't take this anymore. It's much too dangerous for me to be alone on the top floor with the bombs falling all around."

Several hours later, when she heard the signal, Laurette once again climbed the long staircase up to the small apartment. She gathered a change of clothes and some essentials and set off downstairs to the apartment of her friend from school, Marie Frankel. The Frankels had come to live on the first floor of the building after Marie's father was taken away in the train along with Alfred.

"Marie, would you mind if I stayed here with you for a while, at least until this bombing stops?"

"Of course not, we would love to have you stay with us, Laurette. Come, we will set you up to sleep here on the couch in the living room."

The bombing had been going on much of the day and it was already nearly 10 o'clock at night. Marie brought sheets and a comforter and a big soft pillow for Laurette to make herself at home on the couch. As she settled herself down and said "*bonne nuit*" to Marie and her family, Laurette lay for a long time staring at the unfamiliar surroundings. At first she felt more secure. She was with friends and on the first floor. It would be so much safer there. Yet she was still very uneasy. Off in the distance, she could hear an ambulance: "*Dee da, dee da, dee da...*" It was an unsettling sound that often followed an air raid. Laurette tossed and turned for several hours before she finally fell into a restless sleep.

It wasn't quite dawn yet. The sky had just begun to gain a soft pink glow. The rumbling had already begun. It was that familiar sound of airplane engines off in the distance. Laurette opened one eye, then sat up with a start, totally disoriented. In the early morning semi-darkness, it took her a moment to remember she was at the home of a friend, wrapped in a comforter on the living room sofa. She lay back again, unsettled. She stared at the ceiling wondering how close the bombs would fall this time.

The rumbling was coming closer now. Something caused her to glance out into the darkness. She could hear something rattling in the far corner of the room. As she peered toward the sound, trying to focus, she could see the shimmer of a vase, or maybe it was a glass pitcher on the table by the wall.

Laurette pulled the covers closer to her head and burrowed deeper into the cushions, trying to hide herself from the ugly reality of the approaching airplanes. She began to notice a strong vibrating sound coming from the wall directly above her. There was a huge oil painting in a very heavy frame hanging inches from her head. Afraid, she pulled the pillow over her head and waited. The droning of the propellers was coming closer. It seemed the whole room was trembling. There was enough daylight now for Laurette to see the lineup of German warplanes as they swooped past the window–but she did not hear the familiar sound of bombs being released. As the eerie sound of the engines passed by, changing pitch from the Doppler effect as the airplanes grew more distant, Laurette peered from the side of her pillow at the enormous painting above her head.

"If a bomb had hit close by," Laurette shivered, "That picture would have crushed me to death right here!" She decided this was not a safe place for her to stay after all.

As the day grew lighter, Laurette got up and gathered her things. Before leaving, she shared a cup of coffee and a small piece of warm bread with the Frankel family. She thanked them for opening their home to her. Then she explained that her mother had been in need of her assistance and she planned to spend some time with her own family.

Of course the Frankels understood. They also felt a bit sorry for their neighbor who had worked so hard to have her own apartment with her new husband. And now he was who-knows-where and his young bride was struggling to sustain herself through the frightening bombing raids and the many challenges of living in wartime Brussels all alone. Yes, they understood her need to be close to her own family.

What the Frankels didn't know was that there was no room for her in the tiny flat where Laurette's mother and brothers were living. As she sat on the trolley and gazed out the window at the damp, deserted streets, Laurette pondered her predicament. Before the Germans had begun to invade Belgium, Laurette had been studying to be a social worker. Madame Maquinet, her supervisor at the social service office, had been successful in obtaining a scholarship for Laurette to attend *L'École Ouvrière* where she was given room and board as well as a small salary. But the Germans had taken over the school building and her room and board were gone. So now, what was she to do? Her husband had been shipped out to a destination unknown. She couldn't stay in their apartment on the top floor or with her friends downstairs, yet her mother had no room for her either!

Just when she was feeling utterly dejected and lonely, Laurette remembered her friend Annie Davidson. Annie had worked in the radio station with Laurette's dear friend, Louisette. When they were first married Laurette and Alfred used to be invited frequently for dinner with Annie. She made the best macaroni and cheese! They had also dined at Annie 's mother's house, a multilevel building that she had recently turned into a boardinghouse. Perhaps she would have a room where Laurette could stay until things began to get better.

Laurette took the next trolley to the boardinghouse of her friend's mother.

"Madame Davidson, are you sure you have nothing? I have some money that I could pay you." Laurette was nearly pleading. The money she was getting from Social Services was barely enough to live on but it would be worth giving up this small amount in order to have a safe roof over her head and warm food.

"I told you, since the bombing…" her voice trailed off.

"What about the attic?" Laurette insisted.

"Old Madame Masson is staying up in that tiny room in the *grenier* right now."

"I don't mind if she wouldn't mind." Laurette tried desperately to sound genuine, but she couldn't help wincing a bit. Madame Masson had to be at least 80 years old and had foul breath. She always got very close and breathed on you when she spoke. But at least Laurette wouldn't be alone.

"I could help her thread her needles when she sews and fasten the buttons on the back of her dress and…"

"Well, I guess that would be okay." Madame Davidson surrendered.

Laurette breathed a sigh of relief. Now she would feel safe. Her time with Madame Masson would be boring, but dinners in the boardinghouse were bound to be a pleasant diversion. Laurette remembered that when she and Alfred had enjoyed dinners *chez* Madame Davidson, the people dining with them were always interesting and the conversation was lively.

When she arrived at the dinner table, Laurette immediately noticed a gorgeous blond woman who was speaking French with a heavy German accent. As she sat down, Laurette re-introduced herself to the gentleman seated to her right whom she had met previously. He was a military attaché from Siam.

"Bonjour, Madame", he said politely. Then he continued his animated discussion with Helga, the German woman. They were both well traveled and Laurette marveled at their experiences and the places they described. Moments later they were joined by a handsome Russian businessman, an engineer. He sat down next to Laurette and soon they, too, were engaged in delightful conversation.

As Laurette listened to the lively conversations around the table, she munched on the few precious potatoes she was pleased to be able to share with her dinner companions. Laurette loved the local potatoes, which were once in great abundance everywhere in Belgium. But now, they were a precious and scarce commodity because the Germans had taken nearly all the harvest and sent it to Germany with big signs saying "from the thankful Belgian people." Such actions by the Germans infuriated Laurette and many of her Belgian friends. As she was angrily reflecting on the arrogance of the Germans, she became aware that the Russian gentleman had pulled his chair closer to hers.

"Would you care to come to my room to listen to the English radio?" he asked.

Laurette's eyes grew wide. She seldom had the opportunity to hear the news on shortwave radio, since it was illegal for Belgian people to possess such radios.

"I'm sure such an intelligent young lady would be interested to hear what is happening around the world."

Laurette was always desperate to hear the news of the war. Maybe she would learn something of Alfred's whereabouts, so she overcame her initial reluctance.

"Yes, that would be very nice," she responded politely.

As they entered the small room, Laurette noticed that there was just one chair, a small table, an armoire, and a bed. The Russian engineer went over to the radio and dialed in the English radio broadcast. He motioned for Laurette to sit down on the bed. Hesitantly, she sat down on the very edge. When the radio was set, he sat down right next to her.

"You are very pretty," he said softly, taking her hand. Laurette felt very awkward.

Slowly he began to kiss her hand, then her wrist and up the inside of her forearm.

Laurette looked on momentarily in disbelief. The scene struck her as very silly. She had only seen a man kiss along a woman's arm like this in a movie once, and it was a comedy at that.

"What are you doing!" she snapped as she drew her arm away and stood up at once.

"Oh, *Madame*, I am very sorry if I offended you…"

"I must go. *Bonne nuit, Monsieur*," she said curtly. "Good night."

"*S'il vous plait, Madame*, I did not mean to…"

Laurette turned and darted off before he had a chance to complete his sentence. Her heart was racing. She was only a little bit frightened and more than slightly flattered. It had been a long time since a man had flirted with her. She chastised herself silently:

"You're a married woman now, Laurette. Forget about this handsome man and be glad you have found a safe place to stay with good food to eat."

She opened the door to her bedroom to find Madame Masson already snoring.

The next day was Saturday. Laurette walked to the post office, as she did every day, hoping to have some news of her husband's whereabouts. The German soldiers, who seemed to be everywhere these days, eyed her suspiciously as she walked over to the counter. The postman shook his head sadly even before she had a chance to speak.

"Monday, perhaps," he said, trying to sound encouraging.

"*Peut-être,*" she replied as dejected as every other day. "Perhaps."

From the post office Laurette headed over to the Café St. Michel, as she often did on weekends. The café was owned by her friend Chantal and had become a favorite meeting place for many of the German soldiers. Laurette made it a point to spend time there to learn more about the mentality of these strangers who had taken over her home. Most of them spoke only German, which was very difficult for her to understand. Many of the words were similar to Flemish, which she was required to study in school. However, Flemish was a subject Laurette had hated, so she had not learned much of the language. Now she wished she had studied harder.

As she listened carefully to the words and intonations, she was able to pick up the fact that many of these young German soldiers were not particularly fond of their uniforms. As she approached the table where they were seated together with a few of her Belgian acquaintances, one of the soldiers ventured some French.

"*Bonjour, Madame,*" he said politely.

In his broken French and her tiny bit of German, they managed a pretty good conversation. Before long the group was discussing politics. Laurette was feeling comfortable and grateful, once again, for the opportunity to partake in some lively dialogue. As they were chatting, someone mentioned the name Goering, and Laurette made a face. She knew he was a Nazi and somehow closely associated with Adolf Hitler.

"I don't know who he is or what he does, but I know he's a *Schweinehund*!"

It meant "pighound", and was the only German insult she knew.

Suddenly the group was silent. The one German officer grew pale. He leaned forward in a menacing way and locked his eyes on Laurette.

"You're lucky you're a nice-looking girl because anybody else I would arrest on the spot and put in jail!"

Laurette swallowed hard. It seemed that no one spoke for an eternity.

"I'm very sorry," she said quietly, turning her eyes away. "I guess I didn't realize what I was saying."

She tried to sound as coy and innocent as she possibly could.

Slowly the conversation began once again. Laurette breathed a sigh of relief and silently promised to keep her opinions about the Germans to herself from now on.

అఁఁఁ

My God, I thought. My mother could have been shot right then. I wonder if the story was as unreal to her when it was happening as it was to us when we listened.

Meanwhile, my father was enduring his own nightmare....

Chapter 15

May 15, 1940
Somewhere in France

The train rumbled to an awkward stop. For a frightening moment, everything was totally silent. No one in the cattle car moved or even dared to make a sound. Then, off in the distance, a few voices could be heard.

"What happens now?" Alfred wondered to himself.

The voices outside were getting louder, closer. There was a commotion, an energy that made this seem different from any of the previous stops.

Suddenly the doors slid open with a bang. As Alfred's eyes adjusted to the light he saw mountains rising up before him. And as he turned toward the left of the mountains he saw water stretching out for miles.

"Where are we?" he wondered. By the sound of the voices, they were still in France. But it had to be very far south in France.

"These must be the Pyrénées Mountains, he realized. "Then that is the Mediterranean Sea! We're practically in Spain!"

"Move forward, come on move!" snapped an officer.

The bewildered travelers marched slowly toward a large gate that read "St. Cyprien." Beyond the gate were hundreds of wooden barracks built on the sand.

"Well, Fredo." Schmidt had moved in behind Alfred. "It looks like this is going to be our home for a while."

"Silence!" scolded a French officer.

"Let's be sure we are in the same barrack," Schmidt whispered.

The officer glared at him and made a motion as if to smack him with the butt of his rifle. Joseph hustled forward and marched with a very serious demeanor. The officer turned in disgust and went on shepherding the rest of the refugees. People were herded into the barracks, a dozen at a time.

"Store your gear in your assigned cabin and assemble in the courtyard in fifteen minutes!"

"I feel like I'm in a military training camp," said Alfred quietly to his friend.

As they were hustled into one of the barracks they looked around in silence. There was nothing there except the roof over their heads and sand under their feet. Each person selected a small space and placed what little luggage they had with them on the sandy floor to mark their spot.

When they returned outside, there were hundreds of people. Everyone gathered around the officials who were standing among many parcels and packages. Finally, one of the officials began to speak in French. His accent was clearly Belgian.

One by one, he called out names. "…Frankel…Kaufman…Liebermann…Rosa…Schmidt…" Each person received a parcel.

Slowly, carefully, they unwrapped their packages. Alfred couldn't believe his eyes. There inside the small bundle was the key to the elevator of his apartment building in Brussels along with his penknife, a few other small valuables and all the money he had brought into the police station on the day they were deported. Everything was there! It was amazing, after the horrible train ride, the horrendous treatment, and now this flea-infested camp; after all that, the Belgians had returned everyone's possessions, exactly as they had promised.

[Historical Note: These refugees were being harbored under a post World War I agreement between France and her allies to "remove" any non-nationals, especially those with German passports, from potential contact with the German government in the event of a German invasion. The arrangement was designed to keep any spies, members of the so-called "fifth column," from infiltrating allied territory and aiding the enemy from within.]

So here they were. With very little to eat, and only an old army barracks in which to sleep, this wretched camp was to become their home.

And although the conditions were miserable, somehow within a few days, a community spirit emerged. Soon, one of the barracks became known among the refugees as the "club." They assembled some old crates in one corner of the cabin to be used as tables and there they would gather to share ideas. They would bring their tin cups filled with the daily ration of weak soup and make this meager meal last for hours as they passed the time telling stories and philosophizing. It was in this makeshift café, amid the hunger, the dysentery, and the loneliness, that they did what they could to retain their spirit and their hope.

CHAPTER 16

October 1940
St. Cyprien

Several months passed. The conditions at the camp were growing increasingly severe. Many of the men had already died from pneumonia or from dehydration caused by the ever-present dysentery.

Hygiene was nearly non-existent. When the refugees were sick with diarrhea they would have to use big empty barrels as toilets. Sometimes, in their urgency, two or three would use the same drum at once! There were fleas everywhere, and most everyone was infested with head lice.

The food in the camp was so scarce that sometimes the inmates would resort to digging up buried garbage to retrieve old bones to chew on. A young German artist from Alfred's barrack made small ink drawings of such scenes and sold them to Alfred.

*Original sketch of men
eating old bones*

*Original sketch of man
sitting on barrel*

In some ways, though, Alfred was fortunate. He had befriended a physician, Dr. Albert Schenker, during the train trip from Brussels. Dr. Schenker had used his influence as a doctor to help get a second portion of soup for Alfred from time to time. This small gesture was significant in helping Alfred to retain his strength through the long days and nights in the camp.

One day, Alfred was helping an old Hungarian gentleman who had been a well-known movie producer and was now living in the barrack next door. The poor man had become so confused during their captivity that he was nearly helpless. On this particular day, he had broken his shoelace and was at a complete loss as to what to do. Alfred had found some old string and was busy tying the old man's shoe, when Joseph Schmidt came running in.

"Fredo, wait until you hear!" His excitement could barely be contained.

"Just a minute," Alfred said as he finished lacing the shoe with the piece of string.

"*Voilà*," he breathed, and finally looked up at his bunkmate.

"Fredo, the word is out that they are reviewing each of our cases during the next few days. They are going to send some of us home!"

Alfred thought about his apartment in Brussels for the first time in weeks. It was another world away, a lifetime ago.

"What are the criteria for release, do you know?" Alfred asked with some skepticism.

"I guess they will let those who have legitimate reasons to return to Belgium go first, so long as they are not a threat for any reason."

"Well, having a Belgian wife qualifies me, I should think," Alfred said with a small surge of hope and confidence.

"I can't wait to see my family." Joseph stared off into the distance as he began to visualize what it would be like to be going home.

The next afternoon, everyone lined up in the courtyard. The officers shouted names.

"Blanchard...Edouard...Liebermann...Mueller...Schmidt..."

Alfred's heart was pounding so hard he could feel it in his temples. Was it really possible he was going home, back to Brussels to his young wife?

Within an hour, the few hundred selected men were loaded onto a train. There was barely enough time to say goodbye and look back at St. Cyprien. Alfred glanced back over his shoulder as he walked past the gates. He could see a friend giving him the "thumbs up" symbol for good luck. Alfred returned the sign and then quickly turned away.

"Let us hope that this war will soon end and we can all go home to our families and friends," he thought to himself.

This time the train ride was not nearly as long or hard to bear as the trip to St. Cyprien had been. The attitude of the soldiers was much worse though. They were rough and cruel.

They pushed and shouted orders at everyone with their guns always at the ready. As bad as the conditions may have been in the camp, they were never treated like this while they were at St. Cyprien.

Alfred had fallen into a restless sleep. He wasn't sure how many hours had passed. Suddenly, the train began to chug slowly to a stop. Alfred was pretty sure they were still in France, but no one knew exactly where. For several minutes, nothing happened. Everyone sat in silence, afraid to make a sound. The doors opened abruptly and several officers stormed in.

"*Allez, allez, vite, vite*! Let's go, hurry up!"

Alfred noticed the sign at the train station: "Bordeaux."

"What the hell are we doing here?" he wondered.

The guards roughly herded everyone outside and marched the 300 or so men down the street and into a French military building. The officers were wearing the red armbands with the black swastika and spoke German to each other.

"Gestapo," Alfred thought to himself. "The Germans have now occupied France, at least this part of France."

He had heard rumors that Hitler had overtaken Paris in June and had apparently made some kind of deal with someone named Petain who had set up a puppet government in Vichy. So certain areas of the country in the south and southeast were supposedly "free France." But it was clear that Bordeaux was under German command. And Alfred knew all too well what these Nazis were capable of.

Suddenly, someone began to run. Alfred recognized Volowski one of the refugees from St. Cyprien.

"I've got to get out of here," he yelled as he ran.

Moments later a shot rang out and Volowski lay dead in the street.

The guard lowered his gun and turned to the stunned crowd.

"Any more of you wish to try this? For any one who attempts to escape, we will terminate two others, do you understand?" he growled.

And to make his point, he grabbed the two men closest to him and pushed them against the wall. For one dreadfully long moment they stood against that wall. Then the guard turned with an evil grin, shoved the two terrified men back into the group and walked off.

Alfred was feeling sick. He took a deep breath and swallowed hard.

"I can't let them get to me. I have come so far already. I *will* make it."

He followed quickly as the prisoners were shoved into the basement of the building by several German soldiers. It was dark and very damp. Everyone was afraid. It was hours before someone brought water and some small morsels of bread.

"Fredo, look!" His friend, Joseph Schmidt, had stopped sipping from his cup of rusty water and was pointing toward the ceiling.

"Look up," he insisted. Alfred followed Schmidt's gaze to a grate in the ceiling where he could see someone walking above. He realized it was a woman, with rather pretty legs from what he could tell.

"Oh, Joseph, you never stop, do you," Alfred chided his friend.

"Of course not, I'm not dead, you know! Besides, those are free feet walking in the street up there. Much freer than we are in this dungeon!"

Schmidt was right. They were truly prisoners now and their only connection with the outside world was the feet walking by on the street above their heads. For many days, those feet would be their only contact with the outside world.

It was so humiliating and frustrating to be treated like common criminals. Each day at the same time they would be paraded into the yard for inspection. The soldiers would taunt and humiliate them, appearing to derive some perverse pleasure from tormenting their prisoners.

And although many of the guards who dealt with the inmates were utterly cold and often inhumane, there were a few German-speaking soldiers who were different. One day, a short, dark-haired soldier who was probably about 35 years old, quietly came down to the basement and began to speak with Alfred and several of the others. He spoke in a hushed tone and kept looking back over his shoulder to be sure none of the other soldiers could hear him.

"Do you remember last week when you were at assembly in the yard and a tall blond woman told of how several of the inmates had raped her?" he had whispered. "Well it wasn't true, as I'm sure you know. The Gestapo ordered us to beat some of you. We knew the reason for the beating was all a lie. We didn't want to do it, but we had to follow orders or we would have been shot ourselves on the spot!"

He looked behind him on both sides, then continued in a hushed tone.

"We made it look very rough, as though we were really beating the men hard, but we were barely touching them. I just wanted you to know."

He dropped his gaze down as he quietly stole back up the stairs.

Alfred felt sorry for the soldier. It was obvious he was as much a victim of the war as the prisoners were.

As he was reflecting on the incredible power of the Nazi mass psychosis, Alfred could hear approaching airplanes. Everyone instinctively hunched over and covered their heads. The screaming of the sirens on the roof of the building came next and Alfred put his hands over his ears and pressed tightly. The high-pitched sound was torture! He would almost rather have been beaten than tolerate that unnerving siren. Day after day the planes flew overhead, and those sirens sent hideous vibrations throughout the building, violating the ears almost to the point of deafness.

As the sound of the planes finally drifted off and the sirens thankfully ended, it took Alfred several minutes before he could hear well again.

"Hey Fredo," came the rather gruff voice of a friend and fellow prisoner named Johan. His friends called him Hans.

"What is it, Hans?" Alfred was aware that his friend spent considerable time late in the evening talking with one of the German soldiers.

"I hear the British have begun to fight back against the Nazis. That's why these air raids have gotten more frequent. Maybe soon we will be able to get the hell out of here and go home, do you think?"

"One can always hope." Alfred tried to sound optimistic. But he knew Hans had a tendency to exaggerate and no one was sure what to make of any news that came from a German soldier.

All of a sudden five soldiers came rushing down the stairs.

"*Heil Hitler!*" one shouted, making the now familiar Nazi salute that looked as though he were trying to stop traffic.

"All of you, upstairs, *Schnell*! Hurry"

The prisoners scrambled upstairs. This was not the usual time to be assembling in the yard. They were all trembling with fear, anticipating the worst. When they were lined up in the courtyard, an officer began to pull people out of line, one at a time. Alfred felt the muscles in his neck grow tense as 25 men were pulled from the line. Schmidt was one of them.

"We have been authorized to send 25 of you back to Belgium. You will board a train at noon tomorrow. That is all."

The officer turned on his heel and strode away as the remaining soldiers shuffled the prisoners back into the basement.

There was a great commotion as the reality set in for those who were about to be freed. And for the others, another stunning blow.

Alfred was happy for his good friend, but filled with anger and frustration for himself. The chosen men were clearly gentile, not Jewish. He was not going home, at least not this time.

"Fredo, I'm so sorry." Schmidt put his arm around Alfred.

"What do you mean sorry, you are going to go home and take care of your family. I'm happy for you."

"Is there anything I can do for you? Surely I will tell Laurette that you are alive and doing everything you can to get back to Brussels."

"Yes, there is something else you can do for me." Alfred pulled the elevator key from his pocket and some money he had stashed away. He had another key as well that he gave to his friend.

Falcons' Flight

"Take these to Laurette and tell her I will try to get out of here as quickly as I can. Tell her to be strong. And give her a kiss for me."

Joseph Schmidt hugged his good friend.

"Don't worry, Fredo, I'll get these to Laurette and you'll be out of here in no time."

"Be careful, Schmidt. You're not home yet."

ప్రిప్రిప్రి

How awful to think that Dad had to watch his friend, Schmidt, go free while he was still a prisoner in a foreign country. There he was, being held in a basement, a dungeon, with very little food or water and in constant fear for his life. And meanwhile, Mom was back in Brussels, struggling to keep herself going despite the oppression of the Germans who occupied Belgium. She still had no idea where her husband was or if she would ever see him again.

CHAPTER 17

July/August 1940
Brussels

Laurette's days went by very slowly. *La Femme Prévoyante*, the organization that ran the social workers school Laurette had attended before the school's building was requisitioned by the Germans, was trying to reorganize. Madame Maquinet, the woman who had helped Laurette obtain the scholarship to study social work, was helping Laurette stay busy. She had given Laurette a list of names of people who had odd jobs she could do that would help the effort to re-establish the school. This work provided small compensation, but it helped Laurette pay for her food stamps and lodging.

At the boardinghouse, the attaché from Siam had gone back to his country. Others had come and gone as well. There was an Englishman and a very interesting couple, a black concert pianist and his wife. At one point, there had also been another black piano player, a jazz musician, with a white woman for a companion. Almost everyone was gone now except the Englishman and the black couple. Even the German woman, who had turned out to be a spy, a member of the "Fifth Column" in fact, had left. And the Russian engineer, who had apologized profusely to Laurette about his improper advances, had gone back to Russia. Laurette had to admit she missed them all, even the Russian, who had managed to bring her some chocolates as a peace offering. Laurette loved chocolates, and they were hard to come by these days.

One especially dreary, rainy day Laurette was making her usual pilgrimage to the post office, with hopes of finding a letter from Alfred. As she approached the building, she saw a vaguely familiar figure standing at the curb. He was gaunt and tired looking, but he had a certain familiar, innocent smile that broadened widely as he saw Laurette approaching. Suddenly Laurette realized who it was and ran toward him with her arms outstretched.

"Schmidt!" She couldn't contain her excitement, even though she was aware of the

Nazi soldiers with guns standing at every corner, and several in front of the post office as well.

"Welcome home," she cried, hugging him. Her arms wrapped around him completely–something she could not have done six months ago when he was a hearty and healthy young man.

"It is wonderful to finally see you, Laurette," he whispered. Before she could ask the question he went on, "Alfred is alive. He is in Bordeaux."

"Bordeaux!" she exclaimed "What…"

"Come with me," he said softly as he put his arm around her waist. "I'll tell you the whole story. But not here."

"Oh Schmidt, I can't believe you're home! How is Alfred? Tell me everything! Has he lost as much weight as you? What is he doing in Bordeaux? Why didn't he come back with you? Is he safe?"

"Hold on, Laurette, hold on. I will tell you everything."

Schmidt had expected a barrage of questions from Laurette. But he wanted to be sure there were no German soldiers or secret servicemen listening to their conversation. He turned to look directly into Laurette's eyes. Then very softly but intently he said:

"First, a question for you. Where are you living? I looked for you at the apartment and I even went to your mother's home."

"I'm staying at Madame Davidson 's boardinghouse." Laurette responded.

"Oh, I see. Is it safe to talk there?"

"Yes, I'm sure we can find a room where we can speak privately."

Once they had found an empty room at the boardinghouse and Laurette had brewed them both a cup of tea, Schmidt began the long story. He tried to leave out some of the more upsetting details without appearing to edit the story. Laurette constantly prodded her friend to tell her exactly what had happened. She was so hungry to know what her husband's life had been like since he left. There were moments when she gasped and allowed a tear or two to fall. But mostly she was wide-eyed and hanging on every one of Schmidt's carefully chosen words.

"Fredo asked me to give you these," he said placing the money and the two keys, carefully wrapped in a handkerchief, into Laurette's cupped hands.

Laurette began to laugh uncontrollably.

"What's so funny?" Schmidt wanted to know.

"After all those times of dragging myself up and down those stairs at the apartment! Now that I am no longer staying there, now you bring me the key to the elevator!" Schmidt laughed too. It felt wonderful to be able to show his feelings openly and enjoy the company and conversation of a friend without the fear that someone might shoot him just because he laughed aloud.

"The money will certainly come in handy," said Laurette as she regained her composure. "And this," she said, turning the other key over in her hand, "I had nearly forgotten."

It was the key to their safe, which held some money that Alfred's father had sent to them as a wedding gift. She knew that by selling that hundred-dollar American bill on the black market she would have plenty of money–enough Belgian francs to help her survive for as long as she had to wait for her Alfred to return.

Laurette hugged Schmidt again and kissed her friend on the cheek as they parted. She whispered for the fiftieth time that day, "Thank God you are home and safe," as if the mantra might bring her husband home as well.

Then she climbed up to the attic and fell into the most restful sleep she'd had in months.

The next day, with high spirits, Laurette went to the bank to obtain the valuable bill from the safe. She had tried to time her visit so that the Nazi guard on duty would be too busy to notice her. No such luck. As she opened the safe, there was a hand on her shoulder.

"*S'il vous plait Madame*, allow me," he said sternly. He reached in for the bill. "Ah, I suppose you wish to exchange this for Belgian francs, *non*?"

"*Oui, Monsieur*," she said meekly.

Laurette realized that now she would get only the equivalent of the official change and that would be very little. Once again, the Nazis and their control had ruined her hopes of establishing some sense of security.

CHAPTER 18

October 1940
Bordeaux

It had been three days since Schmidt had gone home. Alfred was despondent. He was beginning to believe he would never return to Belgium alive. Even the sound of the footsteps rapping on the overhead grate no longer gave him comfort

In the silence of his despair, Alfred heard the upstairs door swing open so far he could see that many of the officers and soldiers were assembled at the top of the stairs. Two of the soldiers marched down the stairs and stood at the bottom as the same Gestapo officer that had liberated Schmidt yelled from above.

"*Heil Hitler*! All of you, gather your belongings quickly and bring them outside–*Schnell, Schnell!*"

The soldiers pushed and shoved everyone up the stairs. This time, they were lined up to exit through the front door and Alfred felt a momentary glimmer of hope. Then his eyes focused on the huge military trucks idling just outside the gate.

"This must be the end," someone whispered.

"They are sending us to our death. After all this, we are now going to die." Alfred could hear the people around him murmuring their despair.

"*Silence!*" the officer shouted.

A hush swept through the group. The only sound was the steady marching of the prisoners' feet, *clump, clump, clump*. One by one they mounted the moving prisons that would deliver them to what they thought would be their final destination.

The air was thick with unspoken words of fear. Many of the prisoners fought to hold back tears. In the distance, airplanes could be heard, and those intolerable sirens began to wail again. Alfred stiffened against the deafening sound. He longed to cover his ears, but like the others, he was not permitted to move his hands from behind his back.

Once they were loaded into the trucks, the doors slammed behind them. Mercifully, the doors muffled the sound of the war outside and eased the pain on the eardrums. But nothing could ease the heartache of these innocent men.

The vehicles lurched forward. The crowded refugees balanced against one another as the huge wheels bumped and vibrated against the road below them. An hour went by and no one spoke. When at last the doors of the truck swung open, they found that they were back at the Bordeaux train station where a train was just pulling in. The soldiers began to call out "Get moving!" as they roughly pushed and prodded the prisoners out of the trucks and into the cars of the train. Alfred closed his eyes as they pulled away from the station, wondering where they were being taken, certain they were now to be killed.

When he opened his eyes again after several hours, Alfred looked out the window and saw a familiar landscape–the mountains, the sea… They had been sent back to St. Cyprien!

Those who had been left behind at the camp ran to greet the returning refugees. People cried and laughed with relief and confusion.

Alfred found it difficult to express what he was feeling. He was certainly glad they had not been sent to one of those extermination camps he had heard about. And he was relieved to be away from the Gestapo and those piercing sirens. Now the filth and meager food at St. Cyprien didn't seem nearly as intolerable as it had before his experience in Bordeaux.

But mostly, Alfred was trying to focus his mind on finding a way to get back to Brussels.

CHAPTER 19

January 1941
St. Cyprien

It had been raining for nearly four solid days and there was mud everywhere. The smell of mildew and mold permeated the air. Some of the barracks nearest the Mediterranean Sea were knee deep in mucky water, so those men from the flooded-out buildings had to double up in the remaining, already crowded bunks. Alfred and his bunkmates were struggling to plug the holes in the walls and ceilings to keep themselves and the sandy floor as dry as possible. Just then, one of the refugees from another barrack, Harry Brennan, burst into the room. He was panting, his eyes wide with excitement and his hair dripping rainwater onto the floor.

"Alfred, there's a truckload of men going into Perpignan to try to scrounge up some food and supplies. They have room for two more and they're just about ready to shove off. Grab your gear (and your money)," he whispered, "and let's go!"

Alfred jumped up and began to stuff a few valuables into his rucksack. He had never expected that the guards would allow any of the refugees to go into the local town of Perpignan. But security within the camp had been less stringent recently due to distractions caused by the floods. Alfred could see that this could quite literally be the opportunity of a lifetime, and he didn't intend to miss it.

"Hurry, we don't have much time!" Harry insisted as he ran off.

Alfred grabbed his rucksack and ran after Harry, trying not to slip in the pounding rain and mud. They climbed into the military truck just as the engine was turning over. There were nine refugees, one soldier and one lieutenant already inside.

"Lucky thirteen," whispered Harry as he slammed the door shut behind him. "A good omen."

The truck bumped and slid along the flooded roads. Alfred felt swallowed up in the dark interior of this great metal container like Jonah in the belly of the whale, wondering what lay ahead. Alfred didn't know Harry very well, but from what he had heard about the man, Alfred could tell that Harry wasn't the type to volunteer for such a trip without a good reason. Alfred was certain his fellow refugee must have some kind of plan.

An hour or so had passed and they were traveling more slowly. The muddy road had changed to cobblestone.

When the door swung open, they could see that the rain had subsided somewhat. They were parked on the corner near the Perpignan Post office.

As they climbed from the belly of the truck, the lieutenant barked one short command: "Go find what you can and be back in an hour."

It was obvious that the close supervision of the refugees by the camp guards was to be abandoned during this excursion. The urgency of obtaining whatever supplies they could scavenge had superseded the need to watch every prisoner. And though the incessant rains and flooded facilities had caused confusion everywhere, Alfred was still somewhat surprised that the security had become lax enough to permit the inmates to navigate the streets of Perpignan unsupervised. The freedom from confinement felt incredible. To be walking through the streets of a town caused an overwhelming desire in Alfred to be back in Belgium with Laurette and his friends.

When they were a good distance from the truck and outside earshot of the guards, Harry began to whisper his plan to Alfred:

"We're not going back to that place, Fredo."

Alfred wondered what he would hear next. He tried not to react to the arrogant way this person, whom he hardly knew, was now brazenly using Alfred's nickname as if they had been close friends for years. Harry had obviously heard one of Alfred's friends call him by this name. Harry was always bold in that way. But Alfred realized that he and Harry were about to establish a special bond, so he figured he'd better get used to the man's brash ways.

"I've been waiting for an opportunity like this for weeks!" Harry continued. He was whispering now, in a kind of stage whisper for dramatic effect.

"My sources tell me there's a baker in town who's connected with the underground and will hide us for a day or so. When we're sure they've given up looking for us, we'll get the next train out of here. You brought your money, didn't you?'

"Of course," Alfred responded matter-of-factly.

He was not at all surprised to hear that Harry had been making contacts with the underground. Harry had a reputation as a conniving schemer and often bragged about his life before the war. He had been involved in all kinds of financial deals, some with rather unsavory characters. He was also, apparently, quite a playboy. But he didn't have much, if any, money of his own. In his legendary stories, he always hooked up with someone who could finance his schemes. And since Alfred still had some of the money his father had managed to send him, Harry had singled out Alfred as his partner in the escape plan.

"Where will we be headed, Harry?" Alfred prodded, trying to learn as much of the plan as Harry would share.

"I have friends in Lyon," was all Harry would say.

After asking directions to the bakery from a young boy who was bicycling nearby, Harry and Alfred rounded the corner to find a noisy crowd of people standing in line for bread. Harry managed to slide past unnoticed. Alfred followed closely behind, feeling there must be dozens of eyes watching the two of them as they sidestepped close to the wall and ducked behind the counter. Alfred looked back over his shoulder to be sure they hadn't been followed. When he turned back around, Harry had disappeared.

Alfred swallowed hard, trying not to panic. Then he saw a hand gesturing from behind a corner at the back of the shop. He followed the gesture and found Harry scrunched behind one of the huge ovens. Alfred slid in next to his companion.

"I think this will work, Fredo," Harry whispered with a slight grin. "We can hide out here until we know they've gone. Then we'll go and buy our train tickets. You wait here while I let the baker know."

Harry managed to squeeze out and motion to the man behind the counter. They exchanged only a few words before Harry slid back behind the oven next to Alfred.

"We're covered," he whispered.

Alfred felt slightly relieved to know they had found a reasonably safe place to hide. He knew, though, that they were now fugitives and the camp officers would be looking for them. They would have to remain constantly on their guard.

The two men settled into as comfortable a position as they could manage in the narrow space behind the blazing brick ovens. As the minutes passed, perspiration beaded on Alfred's forehead and began to trickle down the back of his neck. He started to feel light-headed--from the heat and the excitement of the escape.

After what felt like hours, they heard a commotion in the shop. A gruff French voice was demanding something but it was unintelligible. Alfred could feel his stomach tighten. Reassuringly, Harry put his hand on Alfred's knee. From the edge of the oven they could see the boots of a *gendarme*, one of the French police. They heard what they thought was the sound of people shuffling out of the way. The bustling sounds of the busy shop became hushed.

"Mais non, mais non, Monsieur. C'est impossible." Alfred could hear a voice he thought was the baker's insisting he had not seen the two men in question.

The boots marched back and forth several times. Then the door slammed shut and the noise level slowly rose from a nervous chatter to the full, animated banter that had preceded the interruption. Alfred began to breathe normally again.

"My guess is he will be back," Harry whispered. "He, or one of his superior officers. We're not out of the woods yet, not by a long shot."

Harry was right. Over the next several hours, right up until the bakery was preparing to close, a series of *gendarmes* came through. Each time, Alfred scrunched himself closer to the wall. Now the muscles in his shoulders were beginning to ache and his legs were getting stiff.

"Come on, Alfred," he chided himself silently, "you've survived much worse than this. It will be over in several hours and then you and Harry will be free," although he wasn't sure just how "free" they would be and what would happen next. He concentrated only on surviving this night behind a baker's oven in Perpignan.

An hour had passed since the shop had closed for the evening. It was dark and very quiet. Harry peered out from behind the oven. The coast appeared to be clear so he began to move about. The street lamp outside the shop provided just enough light to see past the oven. He inched himself carefully along the wall and looked around the corner.

"Fredo, come on out and get some water to drink."

Harry was reaching for a cup above the sink and dribbled some water from the spigot without making much sound at all.

Alfred, meanwhile, was stretching his legs and slowly pulling himself from behind the oven. Pins and needles ran up from his ankles like little spiders climbing up his legs. He limped for a moment until the feeling had returned to his legs. Then he moved cautiously to where Harry was crouched, finishing the last drops of water in the cup. He glanced suspiciously over his left shoulder, then his right.

"Are you sure there's no one lurking in the shadows?"

"We're okay for now, Fredo, but you're right, we must always be on guard."

By this time Harry had refilled the cup and handed it to his companion. Alfred drank gratefully.

"I feel like I've sweated out six kilos behind that oven," Harry said softly.

Alfred nodded agreement as he drained the cup. He had a momentary flashback to the long, terrifying cattle car ride to southern France when a cup of rainwater captured through a hole dug in the ceiling had been equally refreshing.

"Freeze!" Harry whispered suddenly, and both men instantly sucked their backs flat against the closest wall. The beams of two flashlights criss-crossed the room like spotlights. With his peripheral vision Alfred could see the uniforms of two *gendarmes* pacing back and forth outside the large display windows of the bakery. Harry had begun to inch his way back to the oven. As the beams danced off into the night, Alfred slithered back to the oven next to Harry.

"I guess we'd better plan on spending the night here," Harry whispered sadly. "By tomorrow, I'm sure they will have given up on us. They must have more important matters to contend with!"

The two men hunkered down in as comfortable a position as possible to get some rest before morning.

Alfred opened one eye and remembered immediately where he was. His neck was very stiff from having slept sitting up against the wall. The bricks felt cold and hard and he was aware of an urgent need to relieve himself. It was still dark, although he could hear the rustling and chirping of some birds in the trees outside the shop, so dawn was not far off. His joints cracked loudly in the stillness as he extricated himself from behind the oven. Harry stirred next to him and whispered in the darkness.

"What is it Fredo?"

"I'm making a trip to the toilet before daybreak."

"Good idea, I'll follow you."

They fumbled momentarily in the darkness. Alfred ran his hands along the wall until he managed to locate the doorway to the toilet.

On the way back, Harry paused to get a cup of water and a small baguette to quell his growling stomach.

"Not a bad place to hide out, *eh Fredo*?"

He was obviously pleased with himself. Alfred nodded as he downed his own piece of bread.

"I think it will be safe to venture out today," Harry said. "With all the flooding problems at the camp, I can't imagine there will be much more time spent searching for only two prisoners."

Alfred wasn't so sure. "I think we should stay here one more full day," he responded. "The police have already been here several times. They will probably be on the alert elsewhere in town."

"You're probably right," Harry conceded.

As the two men walked about trying to restore the circulation in their legs, they discussed the next steps.

"We'll need to get rid of these flea-infested clothes and buy something new to wear," Harry said. "Then we must get train tickets to Lyon."

"Why Lyon?" Alfred was more curious than suspicious, but he didn't want to take any unnecessary chances.

"I have connections there. Just trust me, Fredo."

At that moment, the front door of the shop rattled slightly. As they hushed and quickly slid back down in their hiding place, the two men heard a key turning in the lock and a long creaking sound as the door opened wide. There was a lighthearted conversation in full swing. The baker and his assistants had arrived for their day's labor.

It didn't take long for the ovens to radiate their extreme heat. Alfred and Harry tried to keep the perspiration out of their eyes. Alfred found that if he concentrated on the good smells and the thought of freedom, the heat was tolerable and the time passed more quickly.

By the end of the workday, no one had come to look for the escapees. When the bakers had finished cleaning and the proprietors had closed the shop for the night, Alfred began to grow restless with anticipation.

"Here's the plan, Fredo." Harry told him. "We stay here through tonight and take advantage of the food and facilities. In the morning when the crowd becomes thick, we exit and find a clothing shop. When we've purchased what we need, we'll find a safe place to wash up and burn our clothes. Then we'll get tickets for the train. By nightfall, hopefully, we'll be on our way!" Alfred nodded, afraid to speak, lest he jinx the escape.

అఅఅ

I could hardly believe the story we were hearing. After all these years, to learn that my father had hidden in a bakery to escape from an internment camp was beyond anything I ever imagined! There were moments that reminded me of scenes from the movie "The Sound of Music." I couldn't wait to hear the next part of the adventure, as I envisioned my father and his companion emerging from their hiding place....

CHAPTER 20

January 1941
Perpignan

It felt wonderful to be out in the fresh air again. Alfred wanted to run, he had so much pent-up energy. But of course he and Harry had to be very careful not to draw attention to themselves. The two men walked as casually as they could into a clothing store. Suddenly, they became self-conscious of how disheveled they were.

Harry, always the charmer, smiled at the proprietor and explained that he and his friend had been visiting friends in the Pyrénées and were caught in the floods.

"Our luggage with all our clothes were completely washed away. We would be grateful if you could outfit us for our trip home to Paris."

Harry could be persuasive, and his native French accent helped a great deal in making his plea sound genuine. The money Alfred took from his pocket and openly displayed to the shop keeper didn't hurt either. Alfred tried to look as pleasant as he could, suppressing a surprised expression on his face when Harry mentioned Paris. He knew they could not leave any clues as to their true destination.

"But of course, *Messieurs*. I would be happy to assist you." The gentleman was politely attempting to avoid wrinkling his nose in response to the odor wafting from his patrons. They, in turn, kept their distance as best they could.

After completing their purchases, the runaways walked briskly with their packages toward the edge of town. Alfred's heart started to race again. They were about to turn a corner to reach a path that led to the woods outside of town when Harry noticed a newspaper in a store window and stopped to buy a copy.

"Good idea, Harry," Alfred said. "We can catch up on the news."

"Yes, and we'll need something to help us start a fire."

They found a small stream and washed themselves in the cold water. Then they built a fire and into it they pitched their lice- and flea-infested garments.

Alfred saw his past go up in the rising flame and smoke. This was truly a new beginning. He dried himself next to the fire and put on the new clothes.

"Amazing how something as simple as fresh clothes can feel so luxurious," he thought.

After dousing the fire, the two men proceeded back into town. The plan had been that they would meet at the train station, which was about 14 blocks away. Harry was to zigzag up and down backstreets while Alfred walked there straightaway. Alfred was to purchase both tickets to Lyon while Harry kept watch. When he reached the counter, Alfred mustered his best French accent and ordered two tickets to Lyon. At that moment, a pretty young girl of about 16 with long, wavy black hair interrupted the ticket-seller and asked him a question. He looked up at her, blushed, and smiled. They exchanged flirtatious words for a moment and then he handed Alfred's change to him along with two train tickets.

The man was still looking at the young girl and bantering with her as Alfred expelled a huge sigh of relief and walked away from the ticket window. He was grateful the ticket-seller had been distracted. Otherwise, assuming someone had warned him of two fugitives from the camp at St. Cyprien, he may have looked at Alfred more carefully and alerted the authorities.

Alfred gripped the precious tickets tightly and proceeded to the far end of the station, where he found Harry smoking a cigarette and engaging in conversation with an elderly gentleman on a bench.

"*Bonjour,*" Alfred said politely to the man as he handed Harry his ticket. "We're lucky, our train leaves in less than two hours."

"Good," replied Harry seating himself next to the old man and returning to their intense discussion of the war. Alfred would have enjoyed participating, but thought it unwise to spend much time with Harry in a public place. Besides, he was too nervous to sit still. So he paced about the train station, watching the people bustling past while planning his next steps to freedom.

When the train to Lyon finally pulled in, Alfred walked purposefully over to the bench where Harry was seated. Harry rose and said "*au revoir*" to the old man.

Harry mumbled under his breath to Alfred, "Stay with me. Whatever I do, follow suit. We must try to stay together on the train if at all possible without being too obvious."

The two men boarded the train. They walked through one crowded car, then a second and a third. They didn't want to sit in an open compartment where an official could walk by at any time and ask to see their papers. Alfred was beginning to worry. Harry walked with great confidence, as always, smiling at the pretty women they passed.

"Always on the prowl, that Harry," Alfred thought to himself.

Harry swung open the door to the next compartment. It was almost completely empty. Simultaneously, the two men realized why. In the compartment was a man in shackles. There were two armed guards seated next to him, one on either side of the prisoner.

"Perfect," whispered Harry. "No one will come looking for us here."

He walked into the compartment and sat down. Alfred followed and together they pulled their new hats down low to shield their faces and settled down in their seats for the long ride to Lyon. For many long minutes, Alfred peered out the window at the world speeding by. Was he really free? He didn't dare believe it. Not yet, anyway.

Lyon–Lyon est la prochaine gare." Alfred heard the sound of a conductor announcing the approaching station off in the distance.

"I must be dreaming," he thought.

He was groggy. The gently rhythmic rocking of the train had lulled him into a deep sleep. He had remained asleep through the long night's trip across France. Harry gave him a nudge.

"Come on, Fredo," he whispered, "Let's get out of here before the guards get suspicious."

Immediately, they opened the door and jumped onto the platform.

"Stick close to me, Fredo," Harry said in a hushed but very excited tone.

Harry was walking quickly and Alfred had to hurry to keep up with the taller man whose long legs gave him an advantage.

"There's our trolley! Hurry!"

They hopped aboard the trolley as it began to pull away.

Alfred was breathing hard, more from excitement than from fatigue. The two men sat down and looked at each other.

"We're almost home, Fredo," Harry said with a broad smile. Alfred allowed his eyes to squint in what was as close to a smile as he'd worn in a long time.

"Can you believe it?" Harry went on, no longer suppressing his excitement, "they never even came in to check our compartment at all!" Alfred nodded his agreement at their good fortune, knowing that it was common practice for each railroad car to be checked by the French Security Police.

"Lucky for us, we had a prisoner on board," Alfred said, realizing the irony of the statement as he spoke. "Now, my friend, where are you taking me? And what time is it, anyway?"

Alfred glanced at his watch. It was just after 8:30 in the morning.

"It's early," Harry replied. "We won't be able to make my contact this early. But I know some places nearby where we can pass the time until then."

Alfred had never seen Harry so animated. He was obviously on home turf here and very glad to be back.

"There it is, Le Café Noir. Let's go have some coffee there."

Harry scrambled out of his seat and nearly tripped trying to jump off the trolley before it had stopped. Alfred hurried after him.

"Here's to freedom," Harry toasted.

Alfred clicked the coffee mug. They both drank silently, relishing the thought.

"As soon as we're settled, Harry, I want to get a message to Laurette."

"Oh, that's right," Harry said apologetically, "I keep forgetting you're married. Sure. We can make the contacts tomorrow to send word through the Swiss Red Cross." Harry, like many others, used the International Red Cross in Switzerland for his contacts because the Swiss were neutral in the war.

Alfred began to let his mind wander. For the first time in eight months, he was confident he would see his wife again. He started to plan how they would make contact with his parents and siblings in America. He had become so immersed in his own thoughts, he had lost track of the story Harry was telling about some of the crazy deals he had gotten into before the war.

"You have family in America, don't you Fredo?"

The question brought Alfred back to his companion.

"Yes, my parents and brother are in Philadelphia. I also have a sister in Baltimore and another in New York City."

"I have an uncle in the States, too." Harry said. "He's a successful lawyer and justice of the court. I don't think he likes to admit he's related to me after all the trouble I've gotten into. I'll bet you don't believe my stories, do you Fredo?"

Alfred paid the tab and hustled his friend out the door, trying to avoid engaging him, knowing his ego was in full bloom.

"I can prove it, do you want me to prove it?"

"Relax, Harry. You don't need to prove anything to me." It was obviously going to be tough to keep his companion from making his point.

"There, I bet they'll have it," Harry exclaimed running toward a magazine shop.

"Have what?" Alfred yelled, running after him, then looking around hoping no one was watching this ridiculous display. But Harry was already in the store, rifling through some of the older journals.

"What are you looking for?" Alfred demanded in his companion's ear as he drew up beside him.

"Wait…ah, here! I knew they would have it!" Harry took the magazine to the cashier and asked Alfred to pay for it.

"Come on, Fredo. I have something to show you. But not here." He began to walk at a very fast pace again, down some narrow streets toward the docks at the edge of the Rhone River.

"I used to love to come down here to think, to get away from the world." Harry got a faraway look in his eyes. Then he snapped back to the present. "Over there, near those steps that go down to the water."

Harry settled himself down by the lapping water. He had to squint in the bright sunshine.

"The sun feels great on this brisk winter day," thought Alfred as he sat down next to Harry. "Now what is all this mystery about?"

He thought Harry didn't hear him as he was madly paging through the journal. Suddenly he stopped and slapped at the page.

"There you are, *mein Freund*!" Harry liked to tease Alfred by saying an occasional word in German. He was using the tactic now to emphasize his sense of triumph.

Alfred looked at the page and his mouth fell open. There was a portrait of Harry, with two gorgeous scantily clad women, one on each arm. The headline proclaimed him "Harry Brennan, France's most infamous playboy and con artist."

Harry laughed as he shoved the magazine into Alfred's hands. Alfred scanned the page in disbelief. He wasn't reading every word, but he could discern that Harry was wanted by the French police on several counts of fraud.

"Yeah, my Uncle Louie is just as glad that I'm far enough away not to cause him any embarrassment in the U.S.," he said, sounding proud in a perverse sort of way. "I guess we'd better get rid of this so no one traces it to us."

Harry began to tear the pages into tiny pieces and toss them into the river.

Alfred thought to himself, "The man may be an obnoxious braggart but at least he's smart enough not to push it to the point of risking our recapture."

They watched the pieces float away and started back toward town. They stopped in the Café Cordon Bleu, where they drank coffee and Harry continued with his storytelling. They talked about the war and politics. They speculated on changes in the political situation since they had been in St. Cyprien. From the newspapers they'd seen and the conversations they could overhear, it seemed that the British were getting more involved and even that America might enter the war. There were more rumors than ever about extermination camps in Poland and Russia. Even the camp where Alfred's father had been, Dachau, had become a death camp for thousands and thousands of Jews who were not wealthy enough to buy their release. Alfred grew melancholy as he thought about his parents who were now in America and safe.

Suddenly, Harry looked around the room, then leaned toward Alfred and whispered: "Sit tight for a few minutes, Fredo. I'll be right back."

With those words, Harry disappeared for 45 minutes. Alfred sipped his cold coffee and waited. He had gotten very good at waiting these past eight months. When Harry reappeared, he was smiling.

"Okay, we're set," Harry proclaimed with a show of confidence.

They settled their bill and walked out of the café, first glancing instinctively around the room to be sure they weren't being followed. They walked three blocks to a trolley stop, their feet making a rhythmic clicking sound on the cobblestones. As they waited for the trolley, Alfred shivered. It was a lot colder in this part of France than it had been in St. Cyprien.

"I sure hope it's warm where you're taking me," he said to his companion.

"I'm sure it will be, Fredo," Harry said with a mischievous smile.

CHAPTER 21

January 1941
Lyon

The trolley Alfred and Harry boarded was very crowded and the runaways were forced to stand a good distance apart. Several times when it stopped to discharge passengers, Alfred had to strain to see if Harry had gotten off. After about 35 minutes, Alfred felt a slight tug on his sleeve as Harry passed him and jumped to the street. Alfred followed quickly.

They walked one city block north. At the corner Harry paused and looked up at a building and smiled. There was nothing distinctive about it, just one more stone building at the end of a row of residences. Rather dilapidated, actually. Harry rang the bell and a voice called out from upstairs.

"*Oui?*"

"I'm here with a friend to see Dr. Charmonte," he called back.

There was a long pause, and Alfred thought he saw someone peak through the lace curtain upstairs. Then there was a buzzing sound and Harry unlatched the door, motioning for Alfred to follow. The smell of strong perfume reached them from far up the long staircase. They climbed two flights to where the stairs were carpeted in red to match the red and gold, oriental-looking wallpaper. A long settee stood in the hallway. Ornate mirrors were hung everywhere. Alfred felt slightly dazed by the surroundings. He had never seen such a place before. He assumed it was some kind of hotel.

A striking woman met them at the top of the stairs. She was tall and buxom with long, very blond, almost white hair piled high on her head and clasped with a pin and fresh flowers. She had a pretty face, though it showed a few more lines than her youthful voice portrayed.

"Please come in and make yourselves at home." She motioned them into the luxurious parlor with plush couches and chairs in a red, black, and gold velvet fabric that matched the oriental wallpaper. "Most of the couples have gone home for the evening," the woman explained.

If he had suspected it before, Alfred was now quite certain he knew what went on in this "hotel."

"You two must be exhausted from your travels. I will prepare you each a room where you can go and freshen yourselves. Dr. Charmonte will be here to see you momentarily. Please sit down and be comfortable,"

When they were alone, Harry whispered, "So what do you think?"

"Well, it certainly is ornate." Alfred remarked as he glanced at the chandelier that hung in the hallway. "What did she mean when she said 'the couples have gone home'?"

"This is a hotel that rents rooms by the hour to couples having 'secret romances,' if you know what I mean." Harry responded with a devilish smile. "Dr. Charmonte is a great underground connection, so I feel sure this will be safe for us. And just think, Fredo, large comfortable beds!" Harry winked.

The owner of the hotel, Dr. Charmonte, was a charming man in his early sixties. While his hair held more salt than pepper, his facial features were those of a man of fifty. He explained that he was a physician who also owned and ran the hotel with the help of Rose, whom they'd already met, and Jacqueline, a petite woman in her late forties with wavy brown hair and green eyes.

Dr. Charmonte and his two women friends were gracious hosts. They offered the weary travelers a simple meal. It was warm and tasty, but Alfred couldn't finish what was on his plate. His eyelids were beginning to get very heavy.

"You two must be really exhausted. " said Jacqueline, noticing Alfred's muffled yawn. "Why don't you go upstairs and lie down for the night."

"I think we will do just that," Harry said as he stood to excuse himself from the table.

"Dinner was delicious," Alfred joined in, "Thank you for your kindness and hospitality."

The bed was indeed large and very comfortable and Alfred was soon fast asleep.

He was awakened by a light shining in his face and a gruff voice directly above him. Someone was shaking his shoulder.

"*Réveillez-vous*, wake up! Show me your papers!"

For a split second, Alfred couldn't remember where he was. The perfumed smell of the room brought his mind into focus. The man standing over him must have been an undercover agent in plain clothes. Realizing the danger, Alfred thought fast.

"I have just arrived today, sir. I left my papers with my friend in the next room. He is a good friend of the lady of the house. I would offer to go in and get the papers, but I believe he is not alone, if you know what I mean."

Alfred motioned toward the closed door on the other side of the hallway. His excellent French was coming in handy now and might just be saving his life.

"*Ah oui, monsieur. Je comprends*. I understand." The officer appeared embarrassed. He turned and quickly left the room.

Alfred was shaking. "That was too close," he breathed to no one. It was nearly dawn before he dropped off to sleep again.

The smell of strong coffee roused him and he bolted out of bed. "I must be late already," he thought, groping for his watch.

It was 6:45. He and Harry had promised to be out of the house by 7:30, before the business day began and the beds would be needed. He met up with Harry in the hallway.

"Did you sleep well?" he asked.

"Just barely," Alfred replied. "I'll tell you about it later."

It was a good thing he waited. As Alfred and Harry descended the long staircase, Alfred looked up and recognized the face of a man walking down the hall on the arm of a lovely young brunette.

"*Bonjour, Monsieur*," Alfred said politely, trying not to show his genuine surprise, as the undercover agent from the previous night walked by.

"*Bonjour*," the officer nodded back and continued on his way, together with his lady friend, to a door at the end of the hallway. They walked in and closed the door behind them gently.

"What a crazy world." Alfred blew a sigh of relief. Crazy indeed.

ॐ ॐ ॐ

Imagine my father hiding from the Nazis in a hotel that rented rooms by the hour! (The thought both surprised and amused me.)

Meanwhile, Mom continued to worry about her husband as she waited through the endless hours in Brussels.

It was with the thought of our parents as a young couple separated by war, so close and yet so far, waiting to make contact, to hear some news, that we had to end our session for the evening. We could hardly wait to re-assemble to hear the next part of the story.

When we again settled in for the storytelling, Mom began with her long hours of waiting anxiously, not knowing if Dad was dead or alive. I could imagine the remorse and the fear she was experiencing.

CHAPTER 22

January 1941
Brussels

Laurette had begun to feel terribly despondent these last few weeks. Every day she would go to the post office and every time she asked, the answer was the same–

"No letters for you today, *Madame*."

It was difficult to keep believing that Alfred was alive and safe. It had been almost three months now since Schmidt had returned with the money and keys. If Alfred were all right, why hadn't he contacted her? And if not (she tried not to think of this), then what was she to do with her life?

She still did a few projects for *La Femme Prévoyante*. But there were so many restrictions, and everyone had the feeling of being under constant surveillance by the Germans. In fact, there were German soldiers everywhere. Day after day you could hear their boots clacking on the cobblestone streets. And ever since the Nazis had taken over her school, Laurette felt they had permeated every part of her life. Food was scarce. Whenever a small amount of meat or milk arrived at the market, people would line up for many blocks, waiting to trade precious food stamps for their small portion.

And when she visited her mother's home, Laurette felt even more miserable. Her brother, Roger, had disappeared the same week that Alfred was taken away. He had told their mother he couldn't possibly stay in Brussels with the Germans invading, so he took off toward France on foot, along with many other young men. Laurette discovered later that he had been roaming for weeks from farm to farm, sleeping in barns and begging for what little food the farmers could spare. Many of those young men died of hunger, disease, and exposure. Others were shot by soldiers trying to clear the refugees from the roadways to make way for the advancing German army.

Roger did survive these events, though, and managed to make his way back to

Brussels about five months later. When he arrived at home, his disheveled clothes were full of lice and mold. He looked like a skin-covered skeleton and was so weak he could barely stand up. Laurette's mother, Juliette, spent three months trying to nurse him back to health on the family's limited food rations. Meanwhile, there was Laurette's brother, Jacques, to feed too. And while Roger's condition was slowly improving, Juliette was beginning to show the strain herself, and there were many things she couldn't really do on her own.

≈≈≈

Mom had never before spoken much about her brother Roger. It must have been very difficult for her to see him in that condition.

She was to learn, much later, that Roger was taken by the Germans late in 1941 and forced to dig trenches on the Russian front. For many months the family was uncertain of his whereabouts and how he was being treated. The last news Mom's family received from Roger was from a prison in Berlin. He never explained why he was there. Then, after 1943, they never heard from him again. To this day, no one knows if Roger survived the prison or if he died there.

≈≈≈

The only bright spot in the lives of Laurette and her family occurred when Uncle Dominique came to visit. Uncle Dominique had been married to Laurette's favorite aunt, Julia, until Julia died several years earlier. He was a gentleman with a pleasant sense of humor. He enjoyed Laurette's mother's company and Juliette always seemed to perk up when he was around. She certainly appreciated his help with the chores and in fixing things around their home.

Laurette remembered how much she had enjoyed Uncle Dominique's visits as a little girl. In many ways, he had been more of a father to her than her own papa. And since he was the widower of her mother's sister, Laurette secretly hoped Uncle Dominique and her mother would decide to marry. Then she would know that her mother and her brother, Jacques, would be taken care of. And that would relieve her of the burden of constant worry over her family's welfare.

Laurette was thinking of Uncle Dominique and her mother as she made her daily vigil to the post office. It was a typical overcast day in Brussels. It hadn't begun to rain yet, but by the feel of the raw January air, Laurette could tell that freezing rain or even snow was in those clouds. She pulled her collar higher against the cold wind. Her mood tumbled even further. She hated the cold.

"I don't know why I go through this every day," she mumbled to herself, "it only makes me feel worse."

As she rounded the corner, the guard at the northeast door nodded at her. Everyone knew her by now. She barely responded with a slight smile and then dropped her eyes. When she opened the door to the post office lobby, the lines appeared longer than usual for some reason. Maybe people were hurrying to pick up their mail before the bad weather set in. Laurette made idle conversation with a woman she met there frequently. They didn't dare talk politics when so many German soldiers were around. So they talked about the little food they had, about children and family members who were far away, and other subjects that were anything but uplifting. When she reached the window, Laurette was prepared for the usual response. Instead, she heard some unfamiliar words.

"*Ah oui, Madame*. There is a letter here for you."

Laurette was certain she had misunderstood. She looked around to see if she was mistaken. "They must be speaking to someone else," she thought.

"*Voilà, Madame*." The postman put the letter in her hand. The letter was from the Swiss Red Cross and it was addressed in Alfred's handwriting! Laurette moved aside to let the next person move up. She was dazed and her hands began to shake. She wanted desperately to open the letter but didn't dare read it in public. She tried to hide her excitement as she stuffed the letter in her pocket but couldn't help smiling at the guard as she passed through the door and into the street. A large wet snowflake touched her nose. She glanced around to see that the road was covered with a thin white dusting like confectioner's sugar on a cake.

Suddenly everything looked beautiful. Laurette hurried to her mother's house to share the excitement of opening her precious letter with her family.

As she descended the trolley steps, she put her hand in her pocket to be sure her treasure was still there. She burst into the kitchen with a huge smile. Her mother was leaning over a big pot of soup on the stove.

"*Bonjour Maman, ça va*? How are you?"

"Laurette, you look like the cat that ate the canary. What is going on?"

"A letter," she exclaimed, "I got a letter from Alfred today!"

"What does it say?" Uncle Dominique joined them in the kitchen.

"I don't know. I haven't read it yet. I haven't even opened it!"

She sat down at the kitchen table, her hands trembling. Her mother handed her a kitchen knife to use as a letter opener.

"Well open it, for goodness sake, don't keep us all in suspense."

She slit the envelope and carefully removed and unfolded the letter. She was almost afraid to read it.

"He's in Lyon," she exclaimed. "He escaped from the camp in the south and took a train to Lyon. He is staying with the contacts of a friend. He is healthy, thank God for that, and he says his father has arranged for us to go to Cuba. He wants me to join him in Lyon and we will then find our way to Cuba from there!"

"Why Cuba?" Uncle Dominique wanted to know.

"I suppose it is because that is the way Alfred's family got to the United States, through Cuba," responded Laurette, now breathless with excitement. "I'm not even sure where Cuba is located, exactly. But I know it's on the other side of the Atlantic, near the United States, so it must be safe. And once we are there, we'll get a visa to the U.S., where we'll join Alfred's family."

Laurette's mother looked thoughtful. "And how will you get to Lyon? That's the first question we need to answer."

"I don't know, *Maman*, but I'll figure out a way."

Her youthful enthusiasm tried to overcome the practical, often pessimistic motherly concern. Laurette's mind began to race ahead to the many details to be considered as she prepared for her trip. Naturally, there was no question that she would go immediately to meet her husband. She wasn't even thinking about the possible dangers.

"*Maman*," she said, putting the letter down for a moment, "there is something I want to ask you, now that I'll be going away."

"Oh, you have decided I see." Juliette knew it was useless to try to dissuade her daughter from making the trip, no matter how perilous it might be for a young girl to travel alone across country borders during a war. Any chance to get away from the German occupation and start a new life was worth the risks, especially for a young wife of twenty.

"Yes, of course I must go, *Maman*. But I will worry about you here all alone to care for Roger and Jacques."

"We're not alone, we have friends, neighbors. And Uncle Dominique is here often," she said, nodding in his direction.

"That's just the point, *Maman*. Why don't you and Uncle Dominique get married?"

"Married! We're too old for that!" She looked very stern, but Laurette thought she might have noticed her mother blushing just a little bit, so she turned to her uncle.

"Uncle Dominique, what do you think about marrying my mother?"

"Oh, I think that would be just fine!" he said with a smile, glancing with affection toward Juliette.

Juliette's eyes grew wide in astonishment.

"It's settled then." Laurette moved right along.

She had no time to waste with silly notions of being too old. She had many details to arrange before her trip, and this would be one less worry on her mind.

In less than a week, Laurette had arranged for the marriage license for her mother and uncle, taken the couple to City Hall for the ceremony and made them a nice dinner to celebrate.

"There," Laurette sighed as she lay her head on her pillow at the end of the wedding day. "Now I know my family will be in good hands while I'm away."

The next steps of her arrangements were not so easily accomplished. Laurette had to travel out of Belgium across the border into occupied France, then make her way to Paris and find a place to stay while she obtained a pass to cross the border into "free France."

Laurette had already been to the Nazi headquarters, the German Command Post (or *Commendature*), several times to get the proper papers to travel out of the country. The lines were interminable. She had gotten to the door before it opened at 7:00 in the morning and still she stood in line for many hours. Then she noticed a fellow student from her days in public school. He seemed to have some influence on the proceedings–and he recognized her.

"*Bonjour*, Laurette, what are you doing here?"

"*Bonjour*, Daniel. I am trying to see the commander about a pass to Paris."

"Come on," he whispered, "I can get you in." In a flash, Laurette found herself at the front of the line, telling her story to the commander. He asked her question after question, his voice in a monotone, his face expressionless. Laurette answered every question without hesitation. Finally he paused.

"*Oui, Madame*, I will give you a pass. Just tell me the address of your husband."

Laurette's heart sank. She had come so close. But she couldn't possibly give them Alfred's address lest they find him and send him back to the camp.

Laurette looked at the commander sadly. "I don't know the precise address, Monsieur," she lied, "I must write to Switzerland to get it."

"I'm sorry *Madame*. Come back when you have the address and we will see what we can do. Next!"

Laurette walked away dejected. She could barely look up from her feet as she walked. Someone was reading a newspaper at the trolley stop and for some reason a small ad caught her attention. It said something about Jews leaving Belgium. She came closer to the reader and asked if she could just look at that one page. He handed it to her and she took it home to read it more carefully.

"Any Jews living in Belgium may leave the country," the ad read.

Laurette's spirits lifted. "If I tell them my husband is Jewish, I'm sure I will qualify."

She read on: "Travelers are not permitted to take any valuables–no money or jewelry."

"No money!" Laurette gasped. "How will I travel to Lyon with no money? But I must find a way. I must try."

Laurette was determined. Somehow she would get out of Belgium and cross over into Free France where her husband was waiting to take her to Cuba, far away from Nazi hate and oppression.

The next morning, Laurette went back to the German Command Post. When she finally got to the front of the line (her friend Daniel was not there that day), she explained to the officer that her husband was Jewish and had been living in Belgium. Now he was in France and, as his wife, she wanted to travel there to meet him. She told the story with great passion. She looked up at the tall soldier pleadingly. With no change of expression, he simply blinked twice, stamped a large "J" on her papers with the stroke of authority and said: "Come back in three days to have this reviewed by a superior officer."

Then with an air of annoyance at having paused too long for this matter, he turned slightly and with a stern voice barked "next" and took the papers of the woman who was next in line.

Again Laurette had to wait for the days to crawl by, and again she went to the German Command Post. She was thrilled to see that her schoolmate was on duty. He smiled warmly as he saw her approach.

"Daniel," she whispered flirtatiously, "can you get me in as you did before?"

"Let me see your papers." He was trying to look official, but his youthful smile was friendly, almost casual. He spotted the "J" and the smile immediately disappeared. He became cold and stiff.

"To the end of the line," he said roughly as he turned away.

Laurette was shocked and hurt. She wanted to say "Daniel, not you too!" But instead she dropped her head low and walked to the end of the line. It was hours before she got to the front of the line and could explain her plight to the superior officer and wait for him to review her papers. She stiffened as she watched him methodically read through every page. His eyes squinted at one point, as if he were suspiciously looking for some hidden, false information. Laurette felt her palms grow moist and acid rise in her stomach. She was prepared for him to tell her to come back another time.

"You do understand, *Madame*, that you may take nothing with you. No clothes, no possessions, no money."

"Yes, sir," she said softly, looking straight into his eyes.

He turned away and Laurette couldn't tell what would happen next. It was probably only a minute or maybe two, but it felt like an hour.

When the officer finally turned back to face her he handed Laurette a pass. His eyes seemed to pierce through her momentarily as he barked: "Keep this together with your papers at all times as you travel."

And that was it! Laurette was on her way. But how was she going to make this long trip with no money? She wanted to feel elated, but instead she was miserable.

"I finally have a pass into France and no way to get to Lyon without money," she mumbled to herself as she walked down the lonely road.

She stood shivering at the trolley station wishing she were anywhere but in this damp, depressing, war torn place. As she looked around, she saw the city that used to hum with vitality, where people once greeted one another on the street and children played in the schoolyards. Now the city seemed to be in a constant state of tension. There were soldiers with guns marching along the streets. Warplanes flew overhead and ambulances would bleat their eerie sirens, *"dee da, dee da, dee da..."*

Markets that used to be filled with fresh potatoes and other local products were struggling to maintain enough staples like flour and sugar and coffee to feed everyone.

As she waited for the trolley, Laurette tried not to look at the crumbling gashes in the wall that had been caused by the German bombing raids. It was like looking at a handsome man with huge scars on his face.

It took all the energy Laurette could muster to climb the steps of the trolley, where she collapsed into a window seat near the back. She stared blankly, remembering a melancholy ride home on the train from Paris when she was so crazy in love with Etienne. It seemed a century ago. That was the only time in her life she had been away from home, and she thought she felt as sad as she ever would. During that train ride, Alfred sat beside her, trying to comfort her as she pined for another boy she left behind in France. And now it was he who was far away in France and she had no way to get to him. She wasn't a little girl any more. She was Alfred's wife. And she felt completely helpless.

Laurette was so lost in her thoughts that she didn't notice the young man who had sat down beside her and was looking at her very closely.

"Laure?" he said very softly, "Is that you, Laurette Deprince?"

She turned to find a pleasant-looking young man with reddish-brown hair and glasses. His head was cocked to one side and his expression was quizzical. A look of recognition overtook them both at the same time.

"It is you!" he said with pleasure.

"Phillipe!" Laurette realized he was another of her classmates from several years back. "It has been quite a while. How are you?" She tried to sound enthusiastic but she was still having a hard time shaking her mood.

Phillipe took over the conversation. "You look terrific, Laurette. I heard you married that guy you were seeing, what was his name? Alex something?"

"Alfred," she corrected.

"He was Hungarian or something, right?"

"Austrian," she corrected again.

"Oh yes, yes, now I remember. He played the violin and the guitar, as I recall. Pretty well, too. Where is Alfred?"

"He's in France and I'm trying to figure out a way to get to him." Laurette launched into the long tale of how he had been taken away in a cattle car to a place in southern France. She talked of not hearing from him for a long time, and how she now knew where to find him but had no way to get there. Laurette played with the truth a little and left out some of the specifics for fear that someone might overhear or that Phillipe might have some Nazi friends. One could never be too careful.

Philippe seemed genuinely sympathetic, though, so much so that he got off the trolley at Laurette's stop and walked with her to let her finish her story. When they reached her boardinghouse, she invited him in for refreshments. They were comfortably seated in the parlor sipping tea when she concluded her story,

"So you see, Philippe, I'm stuck here. I have no way to go through France without money."

"I think I can help you, Laurette."

Her eyes grew wide with hope. "You can?"

"Yes. I have a good friend outside of Paris. His name is Claude Brach. I have access to Claude's bank account here," Phillipe said. "All you have to do is give me the money you want to take with you. I will put it in his account here and he will give you French francs there. It's that simple!"

Laurette looked straight into his eyes. This would take a great deal of trust. Laurette was usually a very good judge of character. And she sensed that she could trust Phillipe. But she didn't know if this Monsieur Brach was truly his friend or if he would replace her money if she actually managed to find him.

"What proof will I have?"

"Let's see." He looked around. "Do you have some kind of note pad I can write on?"

Laurette reached into her small bag and pulled out the only thing she had. She handed him her address book and a small pen.

"How much money do you wish to take?"

She reached back into her purse and drew out her money. It wasn't very much, but it was all she had. She had learned that the only way to feel secure was to keep her valuable things with her at all times. She set aside enough for a train ticket from Brussels to Paris and a little more in case of emergency. She also set some aside to give to her mother before she left. Then she counted the rest and placed the bills in Phillipe's palm.

He folded the money carefully and placed it in his vest pocket. Then he wrote something in Laurette's address book and handed it back to her. He had written the exact amount with the words "please give this money to my friend, Laurette" and he signed it "José" and another Spanish-looking word she couldn't quite read.

Laurette looked up at him quizzically.

"What does this mean?" she asked, pointing to the signature.

"Don't worry," he smiled back. "Claude will know."

CHAPTER 23

January 1941
Brussels

The next 12 hours passed like a blur. Laurette packed a small bag in spite of the strict orders she was given. She paid a visit to Joseph Schmidt and he told her to "take good care of old Fredo."

Then she went to her mother's house and gave everyone a tearful hug. Her mother, always the practical one, insisted she wear boots and her warmest gloves and hat. Laurette promised she would as she wiped a tear from her cheek. She tried to give the money she had set aside to her mother but Juliette wouldn't accept it.

"You take that money with you," she said.

"But Maman, it isn't permitted."

"Hide it!" she insisted. And that was the end of it. When Maman insisted on something, there was no sense in arguing.

Laurette gave her brothers one last big hug. Uncle Dominique put his arm around her and told her to be careful. She nodded and turned to give Maman a final kiss.

Laurette stopped at her boardinghouse one last time on her way to the train station. Reluctantly, she put on the heavy boots and hat and stuffed the gloves in her pocket. She looked around at the old attic room and knew, somehow, that she would never see it again.

Suddenly she noticed Alfred's Leica camera on the bureau. It was his prized possession. An impulse overtook her and she wrapped the camera in her sweater and stuffed it into the small bag she was carrying.

When Laurette finally was about to board the train to France, she expected trouble over her bag. She was ready to insist that she needed the extra sweater and to charm the guard outside into letting her pass without an inspection. But for some strange reason, he said not a word. She walked right onto the train and sat down. As she settled in for the long ride she thought, "If I had only known I would not be searched, I would have brought a lot more with me! Oh well."

The hours rumbled by as Laurette gazed at the bare trees and bushes that sped past the window. She was far too excited to really sleep. She did doze off once but someone at the other end of the car sneezed and, startled, she sat up abruptly. When the train crossed the border into France, it stopped while the officials passed through and examined papers. Laurette clutched her bag tightly, hoping no one would challenge her to open it for inspection–and no one did.

Now that the trip had begun, now that she was finally on her way to meet Alfred after so many months of waiting, the ride through France seemed very long indeed. It was beautiful, though. A lot of snow had fallen and the scene glistened white. The countryside looked clean and untouched by the sufferings of the war. With no idea what lay ahead and a vague sense of unreality, she felt as though she were flying across a fairyland on a magic carpet.

When the train pulled into the station in Paris, Laurette suddenly realized there was no turning back. She gathered her things, descended the stairs, and stood on the platform gazing around, amazed at her own courage in coming this far. Now what? People rushed past all around her. They obviously knew where they were going. Laurette gave herself a little pep talk. She imagined she could hear the sound of her mother's voice saying:

"Now look, you have very clear instructions on what to do. People here speak French, so you will have no problem communicating. So let's go!"

Her friend Phillipe had carefully described the route she must take. She was to find her way to the subway that would take her out of the center of Paris into the northwestern suburban area. The routes were clearly marked and would be easy to follow.

"I sure hope he wasn't just saying that to keep me from becoming frightened," Laurette mumbled to herself.

She made her way underground and found the desired route marked in red, just as Phillipe had told her. Well, at least that part had been easy. She paid the fare and went to stand on the platform, which was nearly deserted. Until then she hadn't really thought about how late it was. She had been too nervous to eat very much before she left. And she was hesitant to eat the small amount of bread and cheese she had brought along, since she didn't know how long it would be before she reached her destination.

Laurette held her small bag close and shivered. This was certainly a different Paris than the one she had visited with her friends in the summer nearly six years before. Then, it was warm and she was in love. She was still a child, and the world was at peace. Now it was bitter cold, the world around her was at war, and she was a married woman, risking her life to be reunited with her husband.

Laurette had to wait about 25 minutes before the underground trolley arrived. As the doors parted and she got on, she felt as if the people on the train were watching her.

"I'll bet I look like a foreigner," she thought. "I'll bet all these people are going home to be with their families. And here I am, only the second time in my life I've been away from Brussels and all alone." She was beginning to feel homesick.

"Come on, Laurette," she chided herself silently, "you're going to see Alfred soon. But first you've got to get yourself to Monsieur Brach to get your money back."

Slowly the subway car was emptying. It had made seven stops since Laurette had boarded and at each station, people had gotten off but no one new had boarded. Now there was just Laurette and an older woman with a tattered-looking brown cloth overcoat and a wool scarf of an old faded scotch plaid tied tightly under her neck. She hunched over slightly as she clung to a bulging sack where a loaf of bread and a few small potatoes peeked out from the top. The woman had obviously gone into the city to shop for food.

Then the conductor announced that the next stop was the end of the line. This is where Phillipe had instructed Laurette to get off. She assisted the old woman with her bag, climbed off the train, and mounted the steps leading from the tunnel.

As she stepped into the fresh air Laurette looked around and noticed the old woman she'd met on the train.

"*Pardon, Madame,*" she said politely to the old woman, "where would I find the bus stop?"

Philippe had told her that the bus would pick her up just a block or so from the subway station and would take her the three kilometers or so to Monsieur Brach's house.

"Oh that bus hasn't run past here for many months," the old woman said with a sour tone. "There's a war on, you know." Then she mumbled something about the Germans that Laurette couldn't understand.

"*Merci, Madame,*" Laurette said dejectedly. She could still hear the old woman talking to herself as she padded away, the snow crunching under her worn boots.

"I guess I'll just have to walk, then," Laurette said out loud to no one.

There was just the one old country road and Philippe had told her to take the bus going west. So she squinted into the angled sun rays of late afternoon and started to walk.

She had walked about three quarters of a kilometer and was concentrating so hard on keeping her pace that she didn't really notice she was coming up on a German garrison until she was standing right next to it. There were several German soldiers on guard, carrying rifles and displaying the familiar swastikas on their armbands. A huge Nazi flag was flying over the courtyard and a German army tank was parked in front of the gate. The whole area was surrounded by barbed wire.

Laurette was frightened. Now two guards who had been talking to one another in German paused and looked at Laurette as she crunched through the snow. One said something softly in German and the other laughed. Laurette kept right on walking without looking anywhere but at the road directly in front of her feet.

"It's not a nice day for walking," one guard called out to her in French with a thick German accent.

Laurette smiled slightly and nodded, all the while keeping her pace and never taking her eyes from the road directly in front of her. She could hear her pulse pounding in her ears. Her breath was making small puffs of mist in front of her nose and mouth. She was past the garrison now but kept praying that these German soldiers would not ask her to stop, or look in her bag or ask her where she was going.

She tried to look as calm and confident as she could. "Just keep walking, Laurette," she said to herself.

She reached up and pulled the back of her collar closer to her neck, adjusted the bag on her shoulder, then stuffed her hands deep into her pockets.

As she continued her pace, she realized the soldiers were no longer watching her and she was well out of range to hear them if they were to call to her. She started to breathe a little bit easier. Her hands and nose were getting cold now. The snow seemed deeper and she couldn't keep up the strong pace she had set at the start of the trek.

Laurette was hoping the place wasn't much further. It was starting to get dark and she was feeling cold and tired. She shivered miserably as she tried to keep from thinking about the risk of dying out there, all alone in the snow.

Just then, off in the distance, Laurette noticed a beautiful large farmhouse. It was perched on top of a hill surrounded by a huge snow-covered field. Smoke was coming from the chimney, making the house look warm and inviting. Laurette was certain this was the house of Monsieur Claude Brach.

She reached the long pathway leading up to the big wooden door. The snow had been so deep in the final approach that she was wet up to her knees and didn't even realize it.

Laurette took a deep breath as she approached the door and knocked softly. Nothing happened. She knocked again, a little more loudly this time. Still nothing.

"Someone has to be home," she thought, trembling uncontrollably from a mixture of cold and fear.

Finally she heard a dog barking and footsteps approaching from within. She saw someone peeking out from the side window. Then came heavier footsteps and the door latch clicked. The big wooden door groaned loudly and there stood a very tall man with dark brown hair and green eyes that peered out from under bushy eyebrows. Laurette gasped slightly. She couldn't take her eyes off the heavy dark beard on this big burly man. She had never seen a man with a beard before. He looked the way she imagined a mountain man might look.

"What do you want?" he demanded roughly.

"Are you Monsieur Claude Brach?" she asked, trembling.

"Tell me what you want!" he insisted.

"My name is Laure Marie Liebermann."

She noticed that he flinched when he heard the German surname. His stare became more menacing.

"I have just arrived from Brussels," she went on. Her voice cracked slightly. "My husband has been held in an internment camp in southern France and he has escaped and is waiting to meet me in Lyon. I have had to travel with no money and my friend told me if I gave him some money he would put it into your bank account in Belgium and you would give that amount back to me here in French francs."

She could see that he was curious but did not necessarily believe her. Suddenly she remembered the address book. She reached into her bag to find it and the man's body stiffened in anticipation of a confrontation. Laurette pulled the small book from her bag and held it up for the bearded man to examine.

"*S'il vous plait, Monsieur,*" she pleaded softly, "you must believe me. I have no place else to go and no money…"

He took the address book from her and read the message, including Philippe's Spanish code name. At that moment a look of recognition swept across his face. He smiled a big toothy grin.

"Come in, come in you poor young girl. You must be cold and hungry! You've come a very long way and there was no bus so you must have walked the last three kilometers! Come in and warm up by the fire!"

Laurette felt relief wash over her as she walked into the warm parlor. The room was beautifully decorated with cherry furniture, including a large old rocking chair that was poised in a perfect spot for curling up next to the roaring fire. A big yellow dog had lumbered in ahead of them. He had been sniffing at Laurette's coat and feet. Now satisfied that she had been welcomed into his home, he flopped down right in front of the hearth and looked alternately at Laurette and his master.

"Let me take your coat," Monsieur Brach said. "I have just prepared some dinner. Won't you join me?"

"Well, I am rather hungry," Laurette admitted as Monsieur Brach hung her coat on a hook in the closet. She couldn't quite believe what had just taken place. In one moment she had gone from sheer terror at meeting this bearded stranger who seemed about to throw her out in the street, to being welcomed as a guest for dinner. After the long days of travel through the cold and snow, the whole situation seemed unreal and dreamlike.

When they sat down to eat, Laurette couldn't believe her eyes. There were freshly cooked potatoes and beans and a small portion of pork. They even had some wine and a few pieces of dried fruit for dessert. Laurette hadn't eaten this well in many months.

As they ate, Monsieur Brach spoke of his apartment in downtown Paris, where his wife and sons were living. He explained how he frequently came to this place in the country to get away from the prying eyes and ears of the Germans currently in power. This was the only place he felt he could safely conduct "his business," which included extensive underground, activities.

Monsieur Brach, or Claude as he asked to be called, then went on to explain to Laurette how he and Philippe had fought together during the Civil War in Spain. That is where he had gotten the Spanish nickname of José Gonzales.

"Ah, now I understand," Laurette said.

The puzzle was finally coming together. Now Laurette felt confident she would receive her money and a pass to travel through to Free France and soon she would be reunited with her Alfred.

She realized how fortunate she had been to run into Phillipe when she did, and to have found her way to the home of Monsieur Brach. While they were drinking a cup of hot tea, Claude explained to Laurette what she needed to do to get to the hostel in the Latin Quarter in Paris. This was where she would be staying until she was able to obtain the required documents to continue her travels.

He insisted that if she had any trouble at all, she should come to him at the *Théatre des Beaux Art*s in Paris where he was the director. Through his many connections, Claude would be able get her through the border between occupied and unoccupied France with the assistance of the Underground. While Laurette was grateful for the willingness of this stranger to help her, she dearly hoped she would not need to take him up on his offer. She had heard far too many stories of the great danger of "underground escapes."

Noting how very tired his guest appeared to be, Claude graciously walked her to the door, helped her with her coat and reviewed the directions to the Latin Quarter.

"I will always be grateful to you, Claude, for your hospitality and your assistance." Laurette said as she stood in the doorway of his home.

Her host kissed her gently on alternate cheeks. Then he looked directly into her eyes.

"Good luck to you and your husband. May you find your way safely out of France together. And don't forget to look me up in Paris if I can be of any further assistance. *Au revoir*."

Laurette set out into the cold January night and managed to make her way to the hostel downtown. The accommodations were spartan and located in a neighborhood that was quite intimidating. But it was all Laurette could afford. And with any luck, she would only need to stay a few short nights before she would be on her way to Lyon to be reunited with Alfred.

CHAPTER 24

February 1941
Paris

Laurette had been in Paris for nine days. She'd gone to the German Command Post every day, trying to obtain a pass to cross over into Free France. On the first day, when she'd made her way to the front of the line, a young, handsome Nazi officer was seated on the other side of the desk. He had sandy blond hair and deep blue eyes that seemed to stare right through her. He examined her papers as he listened to Laurette's explanation for requesting permission to leave occupied France. She tried to sound confident, but she knew her voice trembled as she spoke.

When she finished speaking, there was an unnerving silence. The officer continued to review the papers. Then he looked up and leaned forward, bringing his face closer to Laurette in an intimidating fashion. Finally he spoke, in French, but with a thick German accent:

"Why would you want to run away with a Jew?" he sneered. "Your family is here. If you leave Europe with *him*, you will never see your family again!"

"But he's my husband," she pleaded.

"Come back in a week," he growled. Then he dismissed Laurette with an air of disgust. "Next!" he barked at the person behind her in line.

During the week that followed, Laurette contacted Claude Brach once more and told him of the delay. He encouraged her to wait out the week and check with the Command Post once more. He assured her that he would help her if, after another week, she was still unsuccessful in obtaining her pass.

On the tenth day, Laurette made her way to the front of the line at the German Command Post once again. There she found the same blond-haired, blue-eyed officer.

"Oh no," she thought to herself, "I hope he doesn't give me a hard time." She swallowed, took a deep breath and said her name as confidently as she could: "Laurette Liebermann."

A look of both recognition and contempt appeared on the man's face when he heard the German Jewish name. He turned and shuffled through some files, shaking his head slightly in disgust as he worked.

Then he paused, withdrew a packet of papers and turned back to face Laurette. She was so excited to see the papers, she could barely contain herself. She smiled at him and reached out for the packet. Without saying a word, the officer tossed the papers at her and shooed her away impatiently with the back of his hand. Laurette was momentarily shaken and hurt by his actions. But she quickly brushed the incident from her mind, realizing she had more important things to think about–like arranging for her trip to Lyon.

As she was preparing to leave Paris, Laurette went to say goodbye to Claude Brach. He wished her well, then took her aside and whispered:

"Laurette, when you get into Free France, I want you to send a telegram. You must memorize it exactly. I can not write it down. You must send it to the name I give you and say that 'Daniel is ill and will not be able to come.' Will you do this for me, Laurette?"

"Of course I will, Claude. I will do exactly as you have asked."

"Wonderful!" he said, kissing her three times on alternate cheeks.

"Now be careful and *bonne chance*–good luck."

Laurette boarded the train from Paris to Lyon. She was still overwhelmed by the events of the past two weeks. She couldn't believe she was on her way to meet her husband. As she gazed out the window, she wondered how he would look. It had been nine months since she had last seen him.

Laurette was getting so excited, she could barely sit still. Over and over she re-read Alfred's letter with the brief instructions. Then she stashed it in a place where she was sure no one would find it, inside her bra.

"Let's see, I must take the trolley to the fifth stop. Then I walk one block north. It is the building on the northwest corner, number 16."

As she climbed off the trolley and headed up the block, Laurette's stomach began to knot and her mouth felt dry. She stopped in front of the somewhat dilapidated building and looked up. It was much like many other residential buildings in that part of the city.

"Number 16," she said aloud, "this is it, I suppose." She pressed the button and a bell rang.

"*Oui?*" she could hear someone say from upstairs.

"*Je suis* Laurette Liebermann," she called back.

A buzzer sounded, then a click. Laurette opened the door and began climbing the stairs. The strong smell of sweet perfume hung thickly in the air and became stronger as she got closer to the top.

An attractive woman with blond hair held way up on her head with a pin of flowers greeted her, saying "Oh, you must be his wife! Come in, come in, take off your coat, and make yourself comfortable in the parlor."

Laurette's mouth dropped open. She had never seen any place like this before, not even in the movies. The red and gold wallpaper fascinated her. It looked oriental, from China probably.

Laurette slipped her coat off her shoulders and handed it to her hostess along with her hat. "Where is my husband?" she asked the woman.

"Oh, he isn't here right now," the woman replied as she finished hanging the garments and closing the door of the coat closet. "He will return in a couple of hours. Would you care for a cup of coffee or tea?"

"Yes, thank you. Tea would be very nice."

"Here is a newspaper and there are some books here if you like. My name is Rose. Please feel at home here."

"*Merci*," Laurette said shyly, taking the woman's outstretched hand.

Laurette sat down, trying to make herself feel comfortable. It wasn't easy, though, in this strange-looking place. She sipped her tea and tried to concentrate on reading the newspaper. But she heard voices and when she looked up, she saw a man and woman walking hand-in-hand. They entered a room down the hall and closed the door. About twenty minutes later, another couple came out of a different room. The man was smiling and saying something softly as he leaned close to the woman's ear. She giggled slightly with a coy look on her face. The couple descended the stairs. Laurette noticed that a maid had gone into the first room and reappeared about ten minutes later with dirty linens. Not more than five minutes after that, an older, distinguished looking gentleman and a young lady about the same age as Laurette walked by and disappeared into the first room where the maid had cleaned. At first, Laurette naively thought these were married couples who were using this place as an accommodation during their travels.

But when a third young woman walked past with a very well-dressed businessman Laurette realized what was going on.

"Oh Alfred, where have you brought me, so far away from my home?" she thought to herself. Then she answered her own question: "To a hotel that rents rooms by the hour!"

Her head dropped back against the cushion of the chair in a gesture of disbelief. She closed her eyes. She wasn't sure how much time had passed. She was having a dream that she was back in Belgium with *Les Faucons Rouges*. They were on a long, lovely hike. Alfred was touching her arm.

"Laurette, Laurette!" She opened her eyes.

"Alfred!" She jumped up and hugged him. They kissed for a long time and then she stepped back and looked at him.

"You have lost weight, haven't you? How much have you lost?"

"Actually, I've put on a few pounds since I've been here in Lyon waiting for you! All I can do is sit in the café all day until it is safe to come back here at night."

"Yes," Laurette said laughing, "I suppose you would be in the way here during business hours."

Alfred smiled. "I guess you've figured out what goes on here."

Before Laurette could reply, Rose walked in with three small glasses of wine. She offered a glass to Laurette and one to Alfred.

"It's time for a celebration," she pronounced. "To the reunion of the bride and groom," she said raising her glass and touching theirs, "and the beginning of your new life together." They took a long sip of wine.

"To our wonderful hostess," Alfred continued the toast, "without whom this reunion would never have taken place."

Laurette felt she must say something too. "To peace," she said quietly.

"Ah yes, to peace," whispered Rose.

సౄసౄసౄ

So, after eight months of separation that were filled with fear and uncertainty, my parents were at last reunited. Thus far, their story had been beyond anything I could have imagined. First, there were the bombs falling on the roof of their apartment. Then there was the image of my father as a prisoner in a holding camp, which I could hardly bear to think of. Finally, there was Mom's story. With no idea where her husband was or what had happened to him, she gave all her money to a mere acquaintance. Then she traveled alone to France only to find her husband, my father, hiding out in a hotel that rented rooms by the hour–with no idea when or if they would ever leave Europe at all. The contrast between the deprivation in their lives and the luxury hotel room we were now sitting in was almost surreal.

In a way, I felt like a child myself, listening to my parents tell me a bedtime story. But this story was real, and I was eager to learn what would happen next. In another way, as an adult daughter of two World War II refugees, I found it unsettling, even frightening, to listen to their accounts, knowing that at any moment they could both have been arrested, sent to a camp, or worse! As Mom went on to tell us how it felt to be reunited with Dad, I tried to imagine what I would have done had I been in her place....

Chapter 25

February 1941
Lyon, France

"What a strange feeling this is," Laurette thought. She was lying in bed next to the husband she hadn't seen in nearly nine months. She could hear him breathing rhythmically. She reflected on the journey she had just completed and the small portion of the story Alfred had been able to share with her of his time in the camp at St. Cyprien, in the garrison basement in Bordeaux, back to the camp, and then the escape. She began to feel as if she were living someone else's life.

The light from under the door provided just enough of a glow that she could focus on the fancy wallpaper. "Imagine! A hotel that caters to people having affairs!" Laurette thought as she looked over at Alfred. "If my mother only knew! How shocked she would be!" Laurette smiled.

Actually, if Juliette had known where they were, she would probably have given them some very stern and practical advice. She would have said something like: "Stay under cover and don't trust anyone. You have a roof over your heads and a bed to sleep in. Use it as your base until you can get out of France. Just be careful!"

Laurette tried not to allow herself to feel homesick or melancholy. Tomorrow there would be much to do. They would go to the travel bureau to see about buying tickets for passage on a boat that would take them to Cuba, and then ultimately to America, where they could join Alfred's family. She fell asleep with the confidence that the worst part of their journey was nearly over.

The next morning the couple rose very early. Their room would be needed for the "business of the day." It was too early to go to the travel bureau so they stopped at one of the cafés where Alfred had spent many hours drinking coffee and waiting for Laurette to arrive. He had tried to keep a very low profile at the Café des Canards even though he knew several of the regular patrons. For a while, they sat, sipped their coffee, and tried to catch up on each other's lives. Alfred asked about Laurette's family. He was also eager to hear how his friend Schmidt was doing.

Laurette began by telling him about her brother, Roger, and how he had left home to escape the Germans. When she described his condition upon his return five months later, Alfred winced and shook his head.

Laurette paused for a moment to look at Alfred. Although her husband had clearly lost weight and his face showed that he had endured much stress, she was grateful that he was not in that same disheveled condition in which her brother had returned home from France. Alfred, in turn, was thinking back to the hours after he and Harry had escaped from St. Cyprien, before they had disposed of their lice-infested clothes. He was infinitely grateful that Laurette had not seen him as he emerged from behind the oven in Perpignan. Eager to move the conversation to happier subjects, Laurette told Alfred of her mother's marriage to Uncle Dominique. Alfred nodded his approval. He had always liked Laurette's Uncle Dominique and felt sure that he would take good care of her mother and her brothers.

In her emotional review of the past months in Brussels, Laurette told Alfred about her meeting with his friend Schmidt upon his return and her surprise and relief to hear that Alfred was still alive. She described Schmidt's skinny and exhausted appearance at first, and his present improvement and weight gain.

"He told me only a few brief stories, Alfred," she said. "I know he didn't want to upset or worry me, but he did describe the way you saved his life with the aspirin in your pocket. I wasn't surprised. You always manage to come prepared for nearly anything." She smiled and touched his hand.

As she looked into his eyes, she wondered to herself just how prepared Alfred had been, emotionally, for the pain and fear he must have experienced during his recent ordeals. At the same time, Alfred was reflecting upon the many aspects of the past months for which he had *not* been prepared. He was certainly not prepared to be hauled off in a cattle car to an internment camp and held for months with scant food and wretched sanitation. He wasn't prepared to be treated as a prisoner, an enemy of people he had never met. He was not prepared for the brutality of the guards in Bordeaux. The needless suffering. The awful oppression. The senseless deaths. But then, who was ever prepared for a war?

Laurette wrapped her hands around her coffee mug. It had already grown cold. She shivered slightly as she gazed at her husband. His face was so drawn and he had dark circles under his eyes. The experiences of the past eight months had clearly taken their toll. She knew Alfred was reluctant to speak about the many trials he had faced since he had left Brussels in that cattle car.

Finally, Laurette couldn't stand to hold back her questions any longer. She began to ask Alfred about the train ride from Brussels to France and about the camp. She wanted to know what had happened when the train was bombed. She wanted to hear how he had been treated by the guards and how he had managed to escape. She was hungry to know everything.

At first, Alfred gave her very clipped responses. It was obviously painful for him to talk about what had transpired. Then, little by little, he began to open up. He tried to emphasize the positive experiences. He spoke of the friends he had made and how they helped to keep each other sane. He recounted how they'd passed the time talking of their families, speculating on the political climate, and sometimes telling some wild stories. He then began to describe his fellow refugee, Harry, and he mentioned the magazine article Harry had shown him.

Laurette was about to ask more questions about their escape from the camp when Alfred hushed her. She realized then how dangerous it was to speak of these things in a public place during a time of war. (Even though the Germans here in France were not as clearly in charge as they were in Brussels, there was still a strong Nazi influence, and the Nazis wanted Alfred. He was still considered an activist against the fascist government. And he had now escaped from a holding camp. So, in a way, he was a fugitive.)

Laurette glanced around her slowly. No one appeared to be close enough to listen. Suddenly, from the corner of her eye she saw a tall, blond-haired man walking toward their table. His eyes were steely blue, and his high cheekbones and square jaw gave him a handsome profile. His shoulders were broad and strong looking.

"*Bonjour,*" he said with a distinct German accent, which made Laurette's muscles tighten with fear. She wasn't sure if he was some kind of German officer in plainclothes or a perhaps even a spy. She had come to be suspicious of anyone who spoke German (except for her husband, of course).

The stranger smiled at her with a broad flirtatious smile. Alfred rose to shake the man's hand and indicated that he was a friend. Laurette breathed a sigh of relief. As Alfred introduced Laurette, he explained that Karl and his wife and two children were German refugees living here in Lyon. Karl seemed to Laurette to be very pleasant and the three of them quickly became involved in an animated conversation. Several hours seemed to fly by before Alfred realized it was time to make the daily pilgrimage–first to the post office and then to the travel bureau.

The lines seemed exceptionally long at the post office and there were no letters for Alfred. He had been hoping for some correspondence from his father. His family had been able to get a few pieces of correspondence to him through underground connections and ultimately through the Swiss Red Cross. Those letters from Philadelphia had become his lifeline. He had already received a little bit of money that had been exchanged from U.S.

dollars into francs by a cousin, Elsa, who lived in Toulouse. This was the money Alfred expected to use to buy the tickets for the trip across the Atlantic.

At the travel bureau the lines wrapped around the block. It seemed that waiting was the only pastime Alfred and Laurette could partake of anymore. Waiting at the café, waiting at the post office, waiting at the travel bureau. Sometimes they would go to the library to pass the time and do some reading. Then they'd return each night to the hotel to sleep. And the next day, there would only be more waiting.

When they were finally able to see a representative at the travel bureau, the Liebermanns discovered that there were no ships bound for Cuba or America which they could board. They were merely told to add their names to the long waiting list and return in a few days.

Several weeks passed in this way. Alfred and Laurette would stand on line for hours only to be turned away with no possibilities of departure. And then more waiting.

One Tuesday morning, the weather had begun to feel a bit warmer. The days were getting longer and the hints of approaching spring seemed to lift Alfred's spirits. He believed something positive was bound to happen on this beautiful day.

When he reached the window at the post office there was a small package for him from his father. As always, Alfred was careful to wear a blank expression to avoid rousing any special interest from those around him. Although there were no German soldiers or Nazi guards on duty there, plainclothes secret police and Nazi sympathizers were ever-present and ready to confiscate money or other valuables at their own discretion. And there was no telling what the Vichy French police might do at any time. Alfred clasped the small package close to his body and walked briskly and confidently back to the library where Laurette was waiting. He went to the men's bathroom where he thought he would have the best chance of opening the package without being observed.

Once inside a stall, he drew an envelope from the package and, to his delight, found two tickets. He tucked them safely inside his coat and set out to find Laurette, whom he spotted at a table between the rows of bookshelves. She was diligently working in her English self-instructional book, practicing some simple English words and phrases in preparation for their trip to America.

He drew a chair up beside her and whispered "I have a package from Papa. I opened it in the bathroom. The package contains two *first class* tickets across the Atlantic on a Portuguese ship to New York *and* an approval for the issuing of emergency United States visas for both of us! Papa worked a long time to obtain these visa approvals through the U.S. State Department. His letter says that he had to appeal many times to President Roosevelt's Council for Refugees because all their quotas have been full for months. I don't know how he did it!"

Alfred imagined it must have taken his father many hours of writing letters and using every lawyer and contact he and Alfred's brother-in-law, John Hirschfeld, could find to obtain these visa approvals. Laurette was barely able to contain her excitement!

"Finally! " she exclaimed in a loud whisper. "I can't believe we will be on our way to America at last!"

"We must go quickly to obtain a Spanish visa so we can pass through Spain to Portugal!" Alfred told her. "But first we will go to the American Consulate to have them issue the American visas."

The couple hurried from the library and merrily boarded the trolley. "I can't believe it!" Laurette said aloud. Then, realizing her exuberance had caused her to speak too loudly, she whispered, "These tickets must have cost a small fortune!"

"Yes, they were expensive, I'm sure," said her husband. Both were thinking how lucky they were that Papa had some money he had managed to keep from the Nazis and take with him to America. They were also glad he had maintained the contacts who were now able to assist him as he worked on arranging safe passage for his son and daughter-in-law. Alfred took Laurette's hand and squeezed it. He echoed her sigh of relief.

"Finally," was all he could say.

When they arrived at the American Consulate, once again they had to stand in line. This time the wait seemed longer than ever before. They were so intent on completing their travel plans and preparing for their departure they could barely manage to wait patiently in line, as they had so many times before.

When they finally reached the front desk, the official looked at their documents and shook his head. "I am very sorry, but I cannot honor this request for visas. You already have visas to enter Cuba, so it isn't necessary for you to have an emergency U. S. visa. I cannot issue another visa to you."

It was true. In anticipation of obtaining passage across the Atlantic for his son and daughter-in-law, Alfred's father had managed to obtain Cuban visas for the couple several weeks earlier. It had been expected that Alfred and Laurette would somehow arrange passage to the U.S. the same way the rest of Alfred's immediate family had passed–through Cuba. But now that they had the tickets directly to New York, the U.S. visas were what they really needed.

Alfred tried to argue. Laurette was so shocked she stood in silence. While Alfred was negotiating with the official, explaining their situation, nearly pleading for him to reconsider, Laurette began to feel sick to her stomach. After all this time and effort and money and feeling so close to being free, now the bureaucracy was holding them hostage.

Alfred managed to talk the official into taking their case under consideration. They would have to return in two days to determine the outcome.

Meanwhile, it was only a week before their ship was to depart from Portugal. They now had to go to the Spanish Consulate for visas to pass through Spain to Lisbon to board the Portuguese ship. Again they encountered long, long lines of people. When they finally sat down with an official, they were shocked to hear her words: "I am sorry but there is no possible way you can go across Spain to Portugal to board this ship."

[Historical Note: Men with German passports, like Alfred's, were prohibited from passing through Spain to Portugal because Germany had an alliance with Spain, through the dictator, Francisco Franco. Although Franco was able to maintain the status of Spain as a non-belligerent throughout the war, he had an agreement with Germany to prohibit the possible escape of young German men of military age who might attempt to flee Europe through Spain.]

Unaware of the reason for the problem, Alfred, in his ever-patient calm voice said "I'm sure, *Madame*, that there must be some way to cross through Spain. Perhaps another ship from a different port"

"I'm sorry, *Monsieur*. This can not be arranged."

The war had made every aspect of their life a trial. Now that they were so close to finding a way out, once again they were trapped behind military borders they were not permitted to cross.

Alfred and Laurette finally conceded defeat and walked away from the travel bureau utterly dejected. Now what were they to do? Those expensive tickets and visa approvals would be wasted, and they had no other way to leave Europe.

Several more weeks passed. Money was getting low. So were their spirits. The Liebermanns spent most of their time at the library or slowly sipping coffee or tea at one of the local cafés. Occasionally they would meet a friend or acquaintance who would help them pass the time.

One day Laurette was talking with Karl as she waited at the Café des Canards for Alfred to return from the post office. She was careful to have only one cup of coffee– with their funds dwindling, Laurette had learned to make a single cup last nearly all afternoon.

Alfred walked in with a very slight glimmer in his eye. Laurette was probably the only one to notice–he was still so careful not to smile.

"What is going on, Fredo?" asked Karl innocently as Alfred joined them. Karl and his family had become trusted friends over the many weeks they had spent together at the café.

"Good news," Alfred responded. "We have received some additional funds from Papa today."

"That's wonderful!" said Laurette smiling and looking somewhat relieved.

"In francs?" asked Karl.

"No, in American dollars," he replied.

"If you need to make an exchange, I have a good contact for you," said Karl. He wrote a name on a slip of paper and Alfred took it gratefully. He pocketed the paper quickly. He knew this contact would be someone in the underground who would exchange the dollars on the black market for a much better rate than he'd otherwise receive.

"*Danke schön*," Alfred said softly in his and Karl's native language.

Karl's contact turned out to be very helpful and the francs eventually were used to purchase tickets on a French freighter that was traveling to Martinique, a French island in the Caribbean, by way of Morocco. From there it would be a short trip to Cuba where they would arrange for a United States visa.

Alfred and Laurette were happily making arrangements to take a train to Marseilles, the port city from which their ship was to depart. Once these arrangements were settled, the couple set out for the travel bureau to pick up the tickets for the voyage. Laurette was reviewing all the preparations in her mind as she and Alfred walked from the trolley station to the travel office on the corner. She thought about how prudent Alfred was to use the money from Papa to purchase some valuable stamps. This was a safety measure they had learned from other refugees, since it was not possible to carry cash without having it confiscated by the authorities.

As they waited in line, Laurette noticed the two plainclothesmen who often stood near the door. She suspected they were secret agents of some kind. Suddenly, one of the men came walking directly toward her. Her shoulders stiffened. Then she saw the other man turn in her direction. She tried to smile casually, even though her heart was pounding so hard she was sure they could see it beating through her blouse. She held her breath as the first man stopped suddenly and placed his hands on the arms of a man and woman directly in front of where she and Alfred were standing. Goosebumps crept up Laurette's neck.

Words were exchanged quickly as the "secret agent" jerked the young man and his companion out of line, forcing the couple to hold their hands clasped behind their backs. Laurette thought she saw the agent holding a gun. The other agent shoved the woman in front of him gruffly and then pushed them both out the door. No one knew what had happened. But the remaining people in line were very hushed and shaken. It was not the first time that Laurette and Alfred had seen someone nearby harassed and arrested in this way. Yet, each time she witnessed this kind of incident Laurette was very upset. Alfred took her hand and squeezed it to try to comfort her.

Laurette was still shaking slightly as they walked to the desk to obtain the tickets. She had a sickening feeling in her stomach.

The gentleman leaned forward with a subtle grin and handed her one ticket. She gave him a puzzled look.

"We were to receive two tickets, one for me and one for my husband" she said, nodding toward Alfred.

"*Je regrette, Madame*. I am sorry. This ticket is for you only. That is all." He began to dismiss them and call the next person in line.

"No, you don't understand. I cannot leave France without my husband. We have paid for two tickets."

"*Non, Madame*, I am sorry. There is only one ticket here for you alone."

"Then we want our money back!" she demanded.

"As you wish, *Madame*," he said brusquely.

"How could this happen?" Laurette said to Alfred quietly as they took the money and shuffled out the door.

Once they were outside, Laurette began to question herself: "Should I have argued longer with the agent? Should I have insisted somehow? Maybe I should have flirted with him…? Or maybe we could have tried to bribe him!"

"No, Laurette. In fact, I suppose I am not really surprised this happened," Alfred responded.

Laurette looked at him quizzically.

He went on to explain: "I had heard that the travel bureaus were selling tickets for those white trade ships taking girls to Africa. I'm sure that's what they were trying to do."

Laurette felt a mixture of shock and relief. Shock that she might have been shipped to Africa. And relieved to know that Alfred was not completely devastated by this latest setback.

"Now what are we going to do?" she asked of no one in particular.

"We try again," replied Alfred with his usual optimism. "In the meantime, we have been invited to visit with Karl and his family."

Laurette wasn't much in the mood to be sociable. She was frustrated at this most recent setback in their travel plans. And she was weary. The constant feeling of oppression and fear which was reinforced by the actions of the "secret agents" at the travel office, left Laurette somber, almost depressed. Laurette swept her hand across her freckled forehead, as if to brush away the negative thoughts, as she moved her strawberry blond bangs to one side.

"I suppose it would be nice to visit with the Karl's family for a while. Perhaps it will help me feel better." She silently promised herself she would not allow this morning's events to derail their efforts to reach America.

Laurette began to feel better once they arrived at their friends' home. Karl, his wife and two children shared the house with another family which included a 13-year-old boy named Thomas.

Thomas was fascinated with the stamp collection Alfred had brought along. He spent hours studying it while the adults were occupied in an intense conversation about the war, politics, and the Nazis.

As Alfred and Laurette were preparing to return to their hideout at the hotel, Alfred took the book of stamps from Thomas. Just as he was closing the last page he noticed that some of the stamps looked different. Upon closer examination, he saw that several of the most valuable stamps had been replaced with stamps of lesser value.

Alfred took the young boy aside. "Thomas," he said sternly, "what have you done with these stamps"

"*Rien*, nothing, Monsieur Liebermann."

"Oh yes, you have exchanged some of these here," Alfred said pointing to the newly placed stamps.

"*Non, Monsieur*, I was only admiring your collection."

"Now, Thomas. You are an honest young man, I know. I am sure you have mistakenly moved these stamps. I want you to replace them immediately and nothing further will be said. Otherwise, I will have to tell your mother and the police what you have done." Alfred stared at the boy harshly.

Slowly, Thomas turned and walked away. A moment later he returned with a stamp book of his own. Without a word, he took the stamp collection that Alfred was holding and quickly replaced the stolen stamps into the compartments where they belonged.

"Thank you, Thomas" he said. "I will not tell anyone about this incident." The boy smiled meekly.

Two weeks later after much perseverance and patience, Alfred and Laurette finally obtained two tickets on a French freighter, the Mont Viso. The ship was scheduled to depart from Marseilles in just eight days and would take them as far as the island of Martinique in the Caribbean. From there, they were assured they would have no trouble finding their way to Cuba.

The couple was excitedly preparing their belongings and saying their goodbyes when there came a knock on their door.

"*Qui est là?* Who is there?" Laurette called through the door.

"Karl," answered a familiar voice. She opened the door and the tall German man walked into the room with intensity in his eyes. "Alfred," he said in an uncharacteristically rough manner. "We have some business to settle!"

"Business?" asked Alfred, genuinely surprised by this sudden intrusion.

"*Ja*. Let us go outside to discuss this." Karl glanced in Laurette's direction and then motioned for Alfred to follow him into the hall. Looking rather perplexed, Alfred followed the man and closed the door, leaving Laurette straining to listen through the wall.

"That money I helped you to exchange several weeks ago. I deserve a just commission and I expect you to pay me now, before you depart from Lyon."

"What are you talking about, Karl?" Alfred had a vague recollection of the recommendation Karl had given him for the exchange on the black market.

"Look, Alfred, I don't want to have any trouble over this. You owe me this money and

I expect you to pay it now."

From behind the closed door, Laurette could hear an occasional word as voices became louder and more irritated.

"Karl," Alfred tried to think quickly," I have no cash now. Everything has been converted to stamps or used to buy necessities for this trip. Look, I have this gold coin. It is from Austria and is worth a great deal of money. More than you've asked for. Take it."

Alfred handed him the coin. Karl turned the coin over in his hand and looked up at Alfred unconvinced.

"That is all that I can give you today," Alfred insisted.

"I'll take this for now," Karl said with a snarl, "but you still owe me cash and I want it in French francs!" He turned and strode away in a huff.

Alfred looked worried as he walked back into the room where Laurette was packing and closed the door behind him. "We must take the earliest train to Marseilles tomorrow, Laurette," he said with great urgency. "I don't trust Karl at all now. There's no telling what he might do. We must get out of here as quickly as we can."

The next morning, Alfred and Laurette boarded the 6:15 train for Marseilles. It was a long ride through the French countryside. Both were relieved to have finally left Lyon. Each was remembering the long train trips that had brought them to that city so many weeks before. And now, they were on their way out of France, away from the war in Europe and thankfully, away from Karl as well. At last they would be sailing to a new country, where they could start over. They would no longer have to be concerned about keeping safe from arrest by Nazi police. They would no longer need to be afraid of both strangers and friends alike. Soon they would be with their family.

Linda Linton

CHAPTER 26

May 6, 1941
Marseilles

When Alfred and Laurette stepped off the train in Marseilles, they were immediately swept up into the bustling atmosphere of the port city. The presence of the Nazis could be felt here even more than in Lyon, since Marseilles was so strategically positioned on the Mediterranean Sea between Italy and Spain. Everyone was acutely aware that the war in Europe was far from over. But, despite the underlying influence of the German Nazis, the Vichy French were in charge and the *gendarmes* (the French police) were everywhere.

Laurette took a long lingering look around. She had never in her life been so far from home. Were it not for the war and the constant fear of capture, she would have found Marseilles a fascinating place to visit. It felt much warmer in this part of France and the smell of the sea was magnificent. Laurette was rather sad that they were to spend only three days in this exciting part of the world.

Alfred and Laurette managed quite easily to find the small hotel that had been recommended to them by the owner of the hotel in Lyon. It was a very modest establishment and their room was so tiny it barely had space for a bed and their few belongings. But it was positioned very close to the dock from which they would be embarking on their ship, the Mont Viso, in a few days.

Once they were settled in the hotel, Laurette and Alfred went to confirm their two spaces on the ship. Since the Mont Viso was a freighter and not a passenger ship, the accommodations would be very simple but adequate, so they were told. The couple was not concerned about the lack of amenities on this leg of the trip. They were simply relieved to have confirmed their reservations and excited that they would finally be on their way to America.

Having settled the arrangements, they went for a walk into the center of town.

Falcons' Flight

Realizing they were very hungry, the Liebermanns stepped into the welcome looking Café de la Mer. Because of the war, food was just as scarce in this part of France as it had been throughout their travels. But fortunately, they were at least able to order a bowl of soup and some fresh bread.

Just as they began on their soup, Alfred overheard a man and his wife discussing their impending voyage on the Mont Viso. The man had wavy brown hair with a touch of gray at the temples and a well-groomed beard. A small puff of white smoke curled from his lips as he absently moved a gnarled pipe from one side of his mouth to the other. The woman appeared to be significantly younger. She had long chestnut-colored hair that fell gently on her shoulders. Her green eyes gazed at her husband with intensity and admiration. Together they looked like a professor with his adoring student. Some of their conversation was in German, some in French, and a few words sounded Polish, which Alfred recognized but could not translate. He leaned over and said *Gutentag* -good day- in German. The gentleman looked up, then smiled hesitantly and said a few words in German. Alfred explained that he and his wife had just arrived from Lyon and were departing for the "New World" in a few days on the Mont Viso. A friendly smile then spread across the face of the bearded stranger and his wife and they asked the Liebermanns to join them.

The rest of the afternoon passed quickly as Laurette and Alfred exchanged excited dreams with their new friends, Viktor and Lynette. Viktor, they learned, was originally from Krakow. His family had moved to Linz, Austria, when he was a child. Lynette, was raised in Switzerland, so they spoke several languages at home. Laurette enjoyed an animated conversation with Lynnette in French while the men conversed in German for hours.

When a fresh round of coffee arrived at their table, Laurette noticed Alfred wincing slightly.

"What is it, Fredo, is the coffee too hot?"

"No, I have a tooth that has been bothering me since we left Lyon. It seems to be worse now."

"I know two brothers who are refugees and are practicing dentistry nearby," Viktor offered. "They are working here illegally and get all their referrals from the underground." Viktor scribbled a name and address on a napkin and handed it to Alfred.

"Well, thank you but I don't think I need a dentist," he replied. He placed the napkin in his pocket next to the aspirin tablets he always carried. He was tempted to take those aspirin but he stubbornly insisted the toothache was not serious.

That night Alfred woke in horrible pain. He sat at the edge of the bed holding his jaw in agony, then began to walk around the bed. There wasn't much room to pace but it was all he could do to keep from moaning. He didn't want to rouse anyone outside their room, though Laurette had been awake with him for two hours already.

"Alfred, did you take your aspirin?" she asked.

"Yes, hours ago," he whispered gruffly.

"Then tomorrow we must take you to those dentists."

Shortly after dawn, they dressed and set out to find the brothers Rubenstein. The ride on the trolley was so painful for Alfred he nearly passed out. Laurette just barely managed to get him up the steps to the front door of number 31 Rue des Arbres. A tall wiry gentleman opened the door and Alfred nearly fell into his arms. Laurette quickly explained who had sent them and the rest of the situation was quite apparent to the young dentist. The brother, who was somewhat shorter and slightly bald, helped to walk Alfred to a large chair in the center of the room. The smaller brother looked into Alfred's mouth and touched a spot.

"Augh!" Alfred grunted loudly. "Uh hum," the dentist responded thoughtfully. He moved aside for his brother to see.

"Yes," said the second brother," it must come out immediately. Monsieur Liebermann, you have an abscessed tooth. We will need to remove this tooth in order to stop the pain."

"Whatever you have to do, please do it quickly," Alfred murmured.

"Madame Liebermann, we would like you to wait here in the hallway, please."

The taller man walked her to the doorway where she was greeted by a kind-looking woman in her early thirties. The woman, whose name was Martine, turned out to be the wife of the taller dentist.

Laurette smiled at Martine, then looked over her shoulder at poor Alfred. She could just see the shorter Dr. Rubenstein bringing something over to the chair next to Alfred. It appeared to be an ordinary pair of pliers! It was at that moment that Laurette realized they had no dental tools and no anesthesia to lessen the pain. Oh God, how awful!

The door closed and Laurette sat down alone in the hallway. There were a couple of books, a magazine, and a three-day-old newspaper. She couldn't concentrate to read–she was too distraught by the thought of what was going on behind that door.

After more than an hour had passed, Madame Rubenstein came out and offered Laurette a cup of coffee. Laurette accepted the coffee gratefully, then watched the woman take a full pot into the other room.

Another 45 minutes went by. Laurette thought she was hearing groans from behind the heavy door. Madame Rubenstein came out to reassure her.

"The tooth is impacted," she said, "and is giving the doctors quite a difficult time. But they are making good progress and it shouldn't be much longer." Her tone belied the optimism in her words.

Another hour passed. Laurette had nodded off into a tension-filled slumber. She awoke with a startled jolt when the door opened again, and Martine peeked out to check on the patient's uneasy spouse. Laurette could see that the two dentists were perspiring and looking very tired. She could not see Alfred's face from where she was seated but she imagined he was barely conscious by now. Then she heard something:

"Aha!" exclaimed one of the brothers. "It has broken off now. The rest will come easily."

About ten minutes later, Alfred shuffled slowly through the door, his face drained of all color, making his eyes appear deeply sunken. His right cheek had already begun to swell. Standing behind him, both dentists appeared exhausted.

Martine helped Alfred with his coat as she gave Laurette specific instructions on how to stop the bleeding and reduce the swelling. Then she smiled and offered them both a word of encouragement. "He should begin to feel much better in a day or two," she said.

Laurette paid the dentists and thanked them all. Then she took Alfred by the arm to steady him as they walked slowly into the fresh springtime air. The couple returned shakily to their hotel room where Alfred remained in bed for the next two days.

The morning of their departure, Alfred was up and feeling much better. Their belongings were all packed and they were nearly ready to head for the dock. Suddenly, there was a knock at their hotel room door.

"Who is it?" asked Alfred, putting his ear to the door.

"It is Viktor," came the voice of their new friend. Alfred opened the door slowly.

"Viktor, aren't you heading down to the ship?" he asked.

"Yes, my wife is outside waiting for me. But I wanted to warn you."

"Warn us about what?" Laurette asked with alarm in her voice as she closed the door behind him.

"I heard some people talking about a man who was looking for you. He was sent by someone in Lyon–Karl or Charles or something like that. He says you owe him a lot of money and he will inform the authorities if you don't pay him before you leave Marseilles."

Alfred glanced over at Laurette who was biting her lower lip, her eyebrows arched with worry.

"There must be some mistake. We don't owe anyone any money," said Alfred, carefully controlling his voice to sound confident and unshaken.

He placed his hand on Viktor's shoulder. "Thank you for your concern. I'm sure this will all be quickly straightened out. Why don't you go down and join your wife and we will see you on the ship!"

Viktor turned to leave. "Oh, by the way, how is your tooth, Alfred?"

"It is gone!" he replied "and I am feeling much better. Thank you for recommending the dentists."

"You are very welcome. We will see you shortly at the dock, then?"

Alfred opened the door for him. "Oh yes, we will be leaving in just a few moments. We will look for you there. *Au revoir*."

Alfred shut the door and turned to Laurette with a long sigh. "That bastard, Karl. I knew he was going to give us trouble."

"Alfred, what shall we do?" Laurette's excitement about their impending departure had turned to grave concern.

"We will go on exactly as we planned. We owe him nothing. I gave him the gold coin, which was much more than he deserved."

"Alfred, your gold coin from Papa?" Laurette was shocked.

"Never mind. Let's get down to the ship. By tomorrow we'll be well on our way to Martinique and we can forget about Karl and toothaches and the war and we'll be ready to start a new life."

As Alfred and Laurette boarded the huge freighter, they began to realize how uncomfortable this trip would be. There must have been at least 300 refugees on board. About half were men and half women. Since the ship was built for cargo, there were none of the usual accommodations for passengers. The passengers had been asked to bring their own portable chairs, which would be all they would have to sit on.

As they boarded the top deck, they were quickly shuffled below where they were assigned crude bunk beds. The men were on one side of the ship and the women on the other. Below them were holds filled with cargo. One hold held cork and the other sulfur, which seemed to give everything a yellow tinge and the awful smell of rotten eggs. Above the holds was a deck which housed the live cattle and sheep that would become their only food. This was definitely not a luxury voyage.

"Oh well, as long as this ship carries us safely across the Atlantic," Laurette thought to herself, "That is the most important thing."

As Alfred and Laurette were preparing themselves to settle in, an announcement sounded from a loudspeaker. "Telegram for Monsieur Liebermann. Would Monsieur Liebermann please come to the upper deck to receive an important telegram!"

Everyone looked around in anticipation. Alfred leaned over to Laurette. "Don't say a word," he whispered. "I'm sure this is one of Karl's tricks."

Again the announcement came, "Monsieur Liebermann, please report to the upper deck immediately!"

From the opposite side of the long room, Alfred could see Viktor and his wife looking over at him. Alfred shook his head slowly and put a finger to his lips to let them know they should say nothing to the authorities. Meanwhile, Laurette tried to look busy, unpacking a few things and trying to make a comfortable space for their travels. An officer came walking through among the refugees, asking questions. Alfred tugged on Laurette's sleeve and backed up behind a pole as the officer passed by.

After about twenty minutes a loud horn sounded from the upper deck and the ship began to move forward. The passengers broke into a spontaneous cheer! They were finally on their way! They were finally going to be free of the Nazis, the Vichy French, the war, and even the betrayal of some fellow refugees.

Chapter 27

May 15, 1941
On the Mont Viso, West of Marseilles

They had been traveling on the Mediterranean Sea for three days. Alfred and Laurette were beginning to know many of their fellow passengers quite well. In fact, Laurette had been singled out on the very first day when group leaders were being assigned. As everyone gathered together on the top deck for the first time, one of the officers walked smartly down the lines of refugees and tapped several on the shoulder. He had been watching the young woman with the strawberry blond hair and overheard Laurette speaking fluent French to the cabin boy.

"*Et vous, Madame,*" the officer had moved her to one side–"you will be the leader of the women in this group."

So Laurette was, from that point on, in charge of a group of fifty women. She was responsible for seeing that they arrived at the appointed time for meals and she supervised the distribution of the soup or whatever small rations her group received.

Little by little, Laurette had made friends with members of the crew. Her fluent French and flirtatious smiles to the crewmembers had won a number of extra portions of dessert for her and Alfred. Sometimes these amounted only to a few additional figs or dates, but with limited rations, every morsel was precious.

One morning, while Laurette was sitting on her portable chair visiting with some new friends on the top deck, she noticed that Alfred had disappeared for a while.

She got up to look for him and found him propped against a railing carefully taking aim and snapping a picture of the cargo in the hold just below.

"Alfred!" Laurette exclaimed, "What are you doing?"

"What does it look like? I'm taking photographs of the ship!"

Alfred was so pleased to be able to indulge in photography once again. Despite the

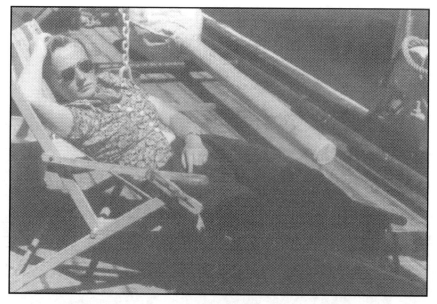

Laurette sitting on the deck of the Mont Viso

Sulfer Cargo aboard the Mont Viso

*Freshly slaughtered beef
aboard the Mont Viso*

Cork cargo aboard the Mont Viso

many times their luggage and belongings had been searched throughout their flight from France, they had managed to hide Alfred's beloved Leica. Laurette had gotten the equipment as far as Lyon and Alfred had protected his precious possession with tremendous care from that point on.

Today was an especially brilliant sunny day. The rays of sunshine reflected from the gentle wake of the ship like shards of glass splitting into thousands of prisms of sparkling light. Alfred lifted the camera and focused on his bride for a profile shot. At the second he pressed the button to release the shutter, he spotted land in the distance!

"That must be Gibraltar!" Laurette exclaimed. One of the crewmembers had mentioned we would pass it today!"

"Close your mouth now, I want a nice profile of you with Gibraltar in the distance," her husband chided.

"Soon we'll be on the other side of Spain," Laurette thought "and then we'll be on our way to America! We're almost free!"

Alfred continued to concentrate on his photographs while all around him there was a buzz of excitement, like a fever overcoming the passengers.

That evening after supper, the conversation was animated. The Mont Viso would be

Profile of Laurette with Gibraltar in the background

landing in Casablanca, Morocco, the next day to refuel and prepare for the journey across the Atlantic. Laurette sat with a new friend, Suzanne Hermann, and her 12-year-old sister, Janine.

"Suzy, I can't believe we will finally be on our way to America!" said Laurette.

Janine's eyes grew wider as she imagined the adventure that was about to begin. "I want to see a camel in Morocco before we leave!" she cried with clear determination in her voice. "I've read about the Arab people and I've seen pictures of them riding atop those huge creatures. I hope we'll see one camel at least!" As she leaned forward with anticipation, those beautiful eyes lit up with youthful energy.

Janine smiled proudly. "I've written a few poems about our trip so far. When we stopped to get fuel in Algiers, I started to write about the people with their turbans and dark skin, and the palm trees, and the strange sounds the women make with their tongues."

Laurette and Suzy smiled at each other as they listened to the exuberance of the young girl. Her chestnut-colored hair was blowing softly with the sea breeze.

It felt so wonderful, Laurette reflected, to be able to enjoy these moments with new friends and to share the excitement of new experiences. What a pleasure to immerse herself in the simplicity of observing interesting sights and surroundings, without fear of being punished for no reason by soldiers and strangers who didn't speak her language. She began to realize the toll this war had taken on her. She hadn't been able to relax and let down her guard for so long. She was just beginning to understand how insidious the oppression of war could be, and what a relief it was to be leaving that oppression behind.

Off in the distance, Laurette thought she could see several dots of light growing larger and brighter. Soon they would be docked at the port in Casablanca.

అఎఎఎ

Ah, so now I know how Mom and Dad met "Aunt Suzy." For many years when I was growing up, I thought Aunt Suzy was really a blood relative of ours. She and her husband, "Uncle Steve," used to come from their apartment in Manhattan to visit us in Philadelphia. And sometimes we would go to New York to see them. It became a tradition for many years for my family to spend New Year's Eve with " Aunt Suzy and Uncle Steve." As I grew older, I learned that they were not blood relatives but very dear friends of my parents. Now I understand why their friendship was so precious. Suzy Hermann, who later married Stephen Friedman and lived in New York City, became a part of my family many years ago on a ship that was sailing the Mediterranean Sea.

CHAPTER 28

May 16, 1941
Casablanca

The next morning, Laurette awakened very early. It was still relatively dark, but she just couldn't stay in her bunk any longer. She slipped into her clothes climbed the ramp to the top deck. As she reached the top and peeked out she could see in the pale light of dawn that a wave of activity was just beginning. As her eyes adjusted to the semi-darkness she noticed that there were a number of other passengers already gathered on deck. They were all just as curious to see the port city of Casablanca. Quickly Laurette lowered herself back down below deck and hurried to the men's bunk area. She tiptoed past half a dozen snoring bodies until she found her sleeping husband.

"Alfred," she whispered. "Wake up and come upstairs with me."

Alfred mumbled and turned over, pulling the small blanket closer to his neck.

"Alfred!" she nudged him. "Come upstairs and see. We're in Casablanca!"

Her husband rolled back and opened one eye.

"Come," she insisted, "get dressed and bring your camera. We're docked in Casablanca!"

"We'll be here for three days," he growled, still half asleep, "there will be plenty of time for taking pictures." Alfred rolled back on his side with his back toward Laurette.

"Oh pooh," she sighed and tiptoed out of the men's sleeping quarters, anxious to return to the upper deck with or without her husband.

It had already grown much lighter. Laurette could see the activity on the pier. Some of the crew were preparing to refuel while others helped to carry cartons over to the market to gather provisions for the long journey. There were many beautiful palm trees along the shore.

While she couldn't make out any faces, Laurette could easily identify the Arab men and women by the white cloth wrapped around them. Most of the men wore turbans and

A street scene in Casablanca

the women were covered from head to foot with draped cloth. She also noticed that some people whose skin appeared to be darker than the others were wearing only black cloth. Laurette remembered reading that the Jews in North Africa always dressed in black.

Eventually, Alfred did appear on the top deck, Leica in hand. The sun was already quite warm, the sky sapphire blue. The port city was bustling with activity while behind it was the exotic landscape of Morocco. It was a photographer's paradise. Alfred longed to get off the ship and take close-up pictures of these fascinating people. Their sun-darkened faces had a warmth and vitality.

And the scenery! There were beautiful palm trees lining the roads and standing by the arched doorways of large white buildings, like bushy-headed guards protecting their fortresses.

Public fountains offered cool water where the women and children gathered to drink

Palm trees along the streets of Casablanca

A Public fountain in Casablanca

A caravan along a dirt road outside of Casablanca

and socialize as they washed the family laundry.

Burros and camels paused to nibble at the low-lying tufts of vegetation while their masters tugged at their ropes or pressed in their heels from atop the beasts.

Small stone walls which lined the roads kept the animals from straying too far in their pursuit of the sparse green leaves and grasses. The dwellings outside the center of town were small and simple. There were no flowers or decorations of any kind. And off in the distance was a beautiful barren beach. Sand for miles and miles.

The passengers leaned over the railings and ropes of the freighter, fascinated by the sights and sounds of Casablanca. There was much excitement and anticipation in the air. Laurette and Alfred talked animatedly with their friends of what it might be like to spend time visiting Morocco, investigating the terrain, and learning of the culture. In reality, though, none of the passengers was permitted to leave the ship while they were in port, and besides, they were all eager to be on their way again. At first, three days in port may have seemed too long, but, in fact, the time flew by.

CHAPTER 29

May 19, 1941
Casablanca Harbor

The atmosphere was electric! Everyone scurried around searching through various bags and suitcases for delicious treasures. One-by-one, cans of sardines, ham, dried fruit, nuts and chocolates began to appear. This was to be a very special celebration as they prepared to embark on the final leg of their journey to the "New World."

Someone in Laurette and Alfred's group had even brought out an old bottle of champagne. It was Dr. Costina, a Spanish surgeon. He was a kind gentleman, though he never seemed to smile.

But tonight was a rare night. Even Dr. Costina appeared to be enjoying himself amidst the rather boisterous celebrations that were going on around him.

As the freighter pulled away from the dock, the celebrants were clinking their various mismatched glasses or tin cups and partaking in the feast of goodies. One of the passengers sang a beautiful song in German. Another told some funny stories about his boyhood in Poland. Janine recited a poem she had written just for this occasion.

Laurette was so busy chatting with her friend Suzy and listening to the others that she didn't realize Alfred had not been sitting among their usual group. When she turned and found him missing, she went to look for him. He wasn't in the bathroom or at the bunks. She began to worry. Then suddenly, she heard the familiar *click* from the shutter of the Leica. She turned and saw Alfred peeking out from behind a smokestack.

"Alfred!" she said in a loud whisper, "what in the world are you doing here?"

"Shhh!" he hushed her as he turned and clicked two more times. She looked out over the water where the camera lens was pointed. There, in the distance, she saw the object of Alfred's photographic frenzy.

"War ships!" She gasped. Indeed, they were warships flying the French flag. Laurette instinctively ducked behind the smokestack with her husband and glanced over his shoulder toward the enemy battleships.

"Alfred, you could get into trouble for this!"

"Shhh!" he hushed her once more, putting his finger to his lips and motioning for her to return to the celebrations. "Keep an eye open for anyone who might come this way, though with all the noise and commotion over there, I doubt anyone will bother."

Alfred suspected he would have another 20 minutes or so before it would be too dark to take any more photos. Laurette went back to the party and told their friends that Alfred was working on a special project and would be joining them shortly.

The partying went on until one in the morning when the revelers contentedly settled down in their bunks to dream of their new lives in America.

The next morning, as light dawned, Laurette awoke with the feeling that the ship was no longer moving. "That's impossible," she thought. "I must have become so accustomed to the motion that I can no longer feel the ocean beneath me."

She wiped the sleep from her eyes and climbed into her clothes. Slowly, she climbed the ramp to the top deck with the growing feeling that something was very wrong. As her head rose above the surface of the upper deck her heart sank. She was looking out over a familiar scene. The port. The palm trees. They were back in Casablanca!

After much commotion the passengers had learned that the British Navy had set up a blockade in the Atlantic that no one was permitted to pass through.

[Historical note: The ship that had launched just ahead of the Mont Viso was captured by the British. It was thought that this refugee ship was carrying contraband. So the cargo was confiscated and the passengers of that ship were sent to a holding camp in England. Since the Mont Viso was right behind that ship, it was ordered back to the port in Casablanca.]

So there they were, back in the Casablanca harbor, docked next to a Belgian freighter that was also stuck behind the blockade. And there was nothing anyone could do but wait.

అఈఈఈ

"Oh no," we were all thinking. "What next?" After jubilantly celebrating their departure for the New World, the ship's passengers awoke to find themselves back where they were the night before!

My parents were now stuck on a smelly freighter that was supposed to be on its way across the Atlantic to Martinique. Instead, they were forced to return and sit in the harbor of Casablanca for who-knows-how-long!

CHAPTER 30

June 2, 1941
Casablanca Harbor

It had been two weeks since the Mont Viso had arrived back at the port of Casablanca. The days dragged endlessly. No one was permitted to leave the ship. The weary passengers did their best to keep busy with what little they had. Alfred often played chess with one of the other passengers. Laurette had already read all the books she had brought along and several others she had borrowed.

They both spent many hours talking with the other refugees and sharing incredible and fascinating stories. Both Laurette and Alfred had become very close friends with Suzy Hermann and her family (her parents, her aunt and her sister Janine).

They also became fond of Dr. Costina and his wife. Madame Costina, they discovered, was the daughter of a well-known judge from the international court in The Hague.

Alfred had taken a particular liking to Dr. Costina. He had noticed on the first day out of Marseilles that the doctor had a peculiar problem with his neck. It was permanently locked in a tight crick so that his head was always turned sharply to one side. It was obviously a painful condition, and Dr. Costina was constantly taking some kind of narcotics to ease the pain. Unlike most other passengers who pretended not to notice, Alfred asked the good doctor how he had come to this uncomfortable state. The doctor launched into a long story, recounting the details of his role in the Spanish revolution against the Fascists. He told of the terrifying experience of standing before a firing squad. At the last moment, someone had saved him from death, but his neck had become locked into this horrendously painful position. Alfred showed genuine concern and sympathy when he listened to this story, which had endeared him to the physician.

One day, when Alfred happened to mention casually that he had been experiencing some troubles with his tonsils, Dr. Costina had insisted on examining Alfred's throat. The doctor, who specialized in surgical procedures of the ear, nose, and throat, strongly recommended that Alfred's tonsils be removed.

"Whenever we're able to get off this ship," said Dr. Costina in a fatherly tone, "I want these tonsils to come out, Alfred. I'll perform the surgery myself. You'll see, you'll feel so much better."

Alfred wasn't so sure. But, perhaps thankfully, there was no way for Dr. Costina to perform surgery while they were stuck on this ship in the harbor of Casablanca.

The days crawled by and the refugees passed the long hours, sharing their stories of the past and their hopes for the future. And waiting. Always waiting.

One morning, Laurette was sitting on deck having a discussion with Suzy Hermann about one of the books she had read. They were both facing the Belgian ship, which was docked next to the Mont Viso. They were barely able to see a couple of crewmembers busily tending to their chores. Suddenly Suzy noticed a small rowboat headed right for the Mont Viso. Several minutes later, she saw a young Arab boy speaking with one of their crewmembers. The boy was apparently asking permission to come aboard. Laurette became as intrigued as her friend, and the two women watched as the young boy boarded the ship and began to walk directly toward them! He had a piece of paper in his hand. He stopped in front of them, handed the paper to Laurette and bowed slightly. Then he took a half step backward and waited for her to read it.

Laurette looked at her friend Suzy with a question in her eyes and Suzy shrugged back that she had no idea what this might be about.

Quickly Laurette unfolded the paper and began to read. The message was in English: "Beautiful blond lady, we want you to come on our boat and have a nice Belgian dinner."

Laurette looked up smiling and glanced over at the Belgian ship as she handed the paper to her friend, who was eagerly awaiting a chance to see what this was all about. Between the two of them, they were able to figure out the English words. Suzy giggled.

Laurette gazed toward the ship, shielding her eyes from the sun with a hand on her brow. As she squinted slightly, she could see three of the crewmembers apparently leaning on mops or broomsticks and gazing right back in her direction!

"Well, well," she thought, "this could be very interesting."

"I guess since my hair is brown," Suzy quipped, "they must have intended this letter for you!"

Although Suzy really wasn't taking any of this very seriously, she was just a little bit jealous of the attention to her companion. "So what are you going to do?" she wanted to know.

"I have an idea," Laurette said with a mischievous smile.

Laurette took out a pen and began to write a response on the note, in French: "*Bien chèrs messieurs de mon pays. Mon mari et moi serions enchantés de diner avec vous. Mais nous sommes prisonniers dans ce bateau, et nous n'avons pas le droit de sortir!"* (Dear countrymen: My husband and I would be pleased to dine with you. But we are prisoners on this boat, and we can't leave!)

She read it over with a look of approval, then showed it to Suzy who was a bit skeptical. Laurette then handed the paper to the young Arab boy and he scampered back to his rowboat and rowed back to the Belgian vessel. Laurette and Suzy looked at each other and began to laugh hysterically! Imagine, flirting with a bunch of Belgian sailors, total strangers, from a distance across the Mediterranean Sea while waiting for weeks in this foreign port. The whole scene struck them as very silly. But it certainly gave them something to talk about now as they whiled away the interminable hours.

They were still laughing about the long-distance flirtation the next afternoon. Laurette and Suzy were taking a brisk walk around the deck and they slowed their pace as they turned to walk along the side that faced the Belgian ship. Suzy squinted and tried to focus on the men who were busy working on the neighboring ship's upper deck.

"I suppose I should be jealous that they invited you and not me," she joked. "I can just imagine how much fun it would be to dine with one of those scruffy sailors!" Her facetious tone couldn't quite hide the genuine jealousy. After all, the refugees on the Mont Viso were restless for a change of scene, something interesting and different to do.

"Oh, I can bet we would eat out of ration cans with our fingers!" Laurette went along with the joke, trying to minimize the special attention she had received.

"Yes and your husband would sit between you and your sailor friend!" They both laughed and chatted merrily as they continued their walk.

Suddenly, Laurette was aware of someone walking directly behind her. She felt a tap on her shoulder. It was one of the crew. "Madame Liebermann, you have a visitor."

"A visitor? I don't know anyone in Casablanca! How could I have a visitor?"

She turned to find standing a few feet away a handsome Belgian merchant marine officer in full-dress uniform.

Laurette gasped slightly and felt light-headed all of a sudden. The officer reached out a hand and walked toward her.

"Madame Liebermann? I am Robert Borrelle, Second Officer of the Frederick, anchored there next to your ship."

He motioned toward the Belgian vessel. To Laurette, the French he was speaking with the familiar Belgian nuances and tones was comforting and familiar, like the lullabies her mother used to sing to her as a child.

She smiled and took his hand. It was warm and strong. He drew her slightly closer so he could speak more softly, privately.

"I am responding to your note. The original message was written by one of my staff.

But, when I saw that your response was in French and you had written 'fellow countrymen,' I decided to come over myself to meet you. I would like to personally invite you and your husband to my ship for dinner. I have already cleared it with your captain."

Laurette was trembling with excitement and disbelief. She turned slightly to look over her shoulder for her friend Suzy. But she had faded into the background and was talking with several other passengers at a distance. No doubt they were all talking about Laurette's handsome visitor.

"*Bien sûr*, of course we would be delighted and honored to join you for dinner," she responded, her eyes sparkling.

"Good then! I will send the young Arab boy at 1900 hours to escort you both to my ship."

He turned on his heel in military fashion, touching the brim of his hat in a kind of salute.

"*Abientôt*, until then," he said with a broad smile and descended to the waiting rowboat.

"*Abientôt*." Laurette smiled back, walking to the rail to watch in awe as the little boat skimmed quietly through the water.

Suzy ran up to join her, together with several of their friends. "Who was that officer, Laurette? What did he want? Are you in trouble? What's going on?" Everyone was talking at once!

"I must go find Alfred," she said, ignoring their questions.

"Laurette!" Suzy ran after her. "Did he really invite you to his ship?" Now she really was jealous.

"Yes. He invited Alfred and me. But I don't really understand why." Then she began to run to find her husband.

Alfred didn't know what to make of this story either. "How did he come to choose you?" he probed.

"I don't know, Fredo. As I told you, a little Arab boy delivered the note yesterday. I responded, more as a joke than anything serious. Next thing I know, we're invited to dine with the second officer of the Frederick!"

"Then we shall dine with the officer!" said Alfred in his matter-of-fact Austrian tone.

Precisely at 7 P.M., the young Arab boy appeared and the couple climbed down into the little rowboat for their mini voyage to their Belgian neighbor. Laurette was trembling with excitement and had to sit down quickly lest she topple the tiny boat!

When they reached the Frederick, Robert was there to greet them, dressed in a shirt and trousers.

"Welcome aboard," he said, reaching out with both hands and kissing Laurette lightly three times on alternate cheeks, as was the custom in Belgium.

Laurette's expression must have shown her surprise at his casual dress. He glanced down for a second, then looked up at her and smiled.

"As you can see, I'm off duty tonight. This evening's dinner is strictly a social affair."

"I would like to introduce my husband, Alfred Liebermann."

"*Enchanté*," said Robert with a slight bow as they shook hands. "I am so pleased you were both able to join me."

His words were genuine. "We've all been so frustrated by this damn blockade. We're bored to tears and anxious to move on. It was one of my crewmen who noticed your wife on the deck of the Mont Viso," he said to Alfred. "I helped him write her a note, not knowing, of course that she was married. When I read the response and realized she was Belgian, I knew I wanted to meet you both myself."

Laurette was drinking in the sound of a Belgian national speaking the French that made her feel instantly transported home.

"So here we are!" he said right on cue as they walked through a doorway into a small private dining room. The table was set with a crisp white cloth cover. Napkins and silverware were neatly placed next to each plate. It was the first time in many months that Laurette and Alfred had eaten a decent meal in a formal setting. It was just beautiful.

Robert poured them each a glass of wine. He toasted "to new friends and to freedom!" Laurette noticed the dimples in his cheeks for the first time. As they sat down to eat, they began to share the stories of the adventures that brought them to this place.

Robert was quite intelligent and very well traveled. He had a fascinating view of the war and all its players. Alfred, whose Belgian accent was still impeccable, was intensely involved in the conversation. He was thrilled to be able to discuss some genuine "news" while escaping the boredom of the Mont Viso. For the first time in ages, Alfred seemed to open up and spoke about the horrors of his captivity in France.

Laurette watched the two men develop an immediate kinship. Robert had a charm that was both strong and vulnerable. He was genuinely touched by the stories he was hearing. At the same time he displayed a wit that had the three of them laughing long into the evening.

The food was delicious and plentiful. There was *bifteck et pommes frites*, steak and french fries! Neither Laurette nor Alfred had eaten such food in a very long time!

"How do you like your Belgian potatoes?" Robert looked at Laurette with a devilish wink, then poured more wine.

"*Magnifique!*" Laurette replied, blushing slightly. She was thinking how sweet and thoughtful of Robert to prepare a typically Belgian meal for her and Alfred.

They talked and ate slowly, enjoying every morsel. Then Robert left the table and returned moments later with strong hot coffee. It smelled divine. He offered a cigarette to his guests, then lit his own and leaned back.

"It looks as if we may be here for a while," he sighed. "The British have set up a blockade in the Atlantic. No one may pass through. How are the conditions over there on that freighter?"

Alfred began to describe the monotony, the close quarters, the limited food.

"Pretty detestable," Robert remarked, "but I have heard worse. I understand there are some miserable work camps set up out in the desert for refugees such as those on your ship."

"I suppose in comparison to what others are suffering, the Mont Viso is not so terrible," Laurette offered. Then, smiling at Robert, she added, "and we certainly have enjoyed this evening with you. Unfortunately, it is late and we really must return to our ship."

"It has been a delightful evening," Robert agreed as he took their hands and held them warmly. "And please, call me Robert. I would be honored if you would visit with me again."

"*Monsieur*, I mean Robert," Alfred quickly corrected himself, "It is we who are honored and grateful for your hospitality. We only wish we could return the favor."

"Would you like to come to the Mont Viso and meet some of our friends?" Laurette asked Robert.

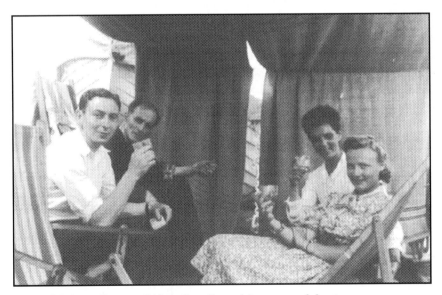

*Dr. and Señora Costina, Robert Borelle and Laurette celebrate
Alfred and Laurette's third wedding anniversary.*

"I'd love to join you. I'm on duty for the next four days. On Friday I have a meeting on shore. Next Saturday evening I would be pleased to join you for a drink if you allow me to bring the wine."

"*Avec plaisir*," said Alfred, shaking Robert's hand.

And so a great friendship began. Alfred and Laurette now had a new enthusiasm for life. And their friends came to know and enjoy the Belgian officer who sometimes joined them on late afternoons and made everyone laugh at his seaman's humor and raunchy jokes.

Robert had even come to the Mont Viso to help Alfred and Laurette celebrate their third wedding anniversary. The new friendship helped greatly to pass the interminable hours at the dock.

Linda Linton

CHAPTER 31

August 1, 1941
Casablanca Harbor

The Mont Viso had been sitting in the harbor at Casablanca next to the Belgian ship Frederick for nearly ten weeks. The passengers were restless and bored. There were always rumors of war events and the chances of being permitted to pass through the British blockade, but they were only rumors.

One morning there was a great deal more commotion than usual on the upper deck. Everyone was rushing about. There had been an announcement just before dawn: "Everyone get up, pack your belongings, and assemble on the top deck with your luggage!"

No one was certain what would happen next, but many feared the worst. They had heard about refugee camps in the Sahara desert. What would happen to them if they were forced to go to one of these camps? It had begun to feel as if they were so close to freedom. And now….

In the early morning light, Alfred and Laurette slowly descended the gangplank and stood on the dock with all the other passengers and their luggage. There were several buses lined up, and one by one the Mont Viso passengers were forced to board the buses that were bound for what they assumed was some horrible place. It was like a death march, a funeral parade.

All at once there was a shout from the dock. An officer was running and yelling *"Attendez! Attendez!* Wait!" Alfred and Laurette had been shuffling forward and paused within several feet of the steps leading onto a bus. They looked around. Laurette felt a strong hand on her shoulder. A rapid argument in a mottled French/Arabic was taking place before her. It was Robert, firing hurried instructions to the officer in charge.

"Non, Non!" the officer was saying and shaking his head. But Robert was insisting. "I

have a room in town for these two people," he argued.

Then he drew some papers from his coat pocket and waved them at the officer. Another official had come over to see what was causing the commotion and delay. Finally, the first officer reached out and roughly grasped Laurette's arm with one hand and Alfred's arm with the other and yanked them out of line.

"D'accord. Ces deux. Seulement *ces deux*! Okay, these two and *only* these two."

And that was it. Laurette barely had a second to swing around and kiss her friend Suzy on the cheek before the Hermann family boarded the bus. They gave a despondent wave out the window as the bus pulled away, leaving Laurette, Alfred, and their friend, Officer Robert Borrelle, standing on the dock.

Watching the last bus leave, the reality of what had just transpired was slowly gripping Laurette and Alfred. Quickly, Robert stepped up to distract his friends from their sadness and the fear they felt for their fellow refugees.

"Come, let's get away from here and find something interesting to do." He put an arm around each of them and smiled at Laurette. They began to walk toward the center of town while Robert spoke animatedly. "I have arranged for you both to stay in my hotel room in town. Since my roommate, as you know, is in the hospital with a very badly broken leg, I will be staying on the ship. I tried desperately to work a deal with the underground police"–he was whispering now–"to get all of you, or at least all the Belgians on the ship into some accommodations so they wouldn't end up taking all of you to the camp. I have been negotiating with the Belgian Consulate for weeks. I am terribly sorry I was unable to help any of your friends," he said with genuine sorrow.

They walked in silence for a time. Laurette and Alfred were taking in the sights and sounds of Casablanca–the dark-skinned people draped in cloth, the bustle of the port city. It was similar to others they had seen but there was something exotic about the whole atmosphere.

Robert's voice broke the silence. "I'm looking forward to showing you around this place. There's a lot to do. But first, we must get you settled, and I need to return to my ship."

When they reached the hotel, they found it to be clean and comfortable. It was also centrally located. Although they were concerned and unhappy about the fate of their fellow refugees, they were grateful for their own good fortune.

৯৯৯

I looked across the room at my sister and brother. We were already considerably older than our parents were during the time of the adventure they were describing to us. I think we could feel their pain as our parents recalled how they helplessly watched their fellow passengers march off to some horrible camp. It was especially poignant knowing our "Aunt Suzy" and her family were among those who boarded that bus.

And yet, at the same time, there was an undertone of excitement and adventure as Mom and Dad went on to relate the highlights of their stay in Casablanca. Certainly, I had never been to Morocco, so my frame of reference was somewhat limited. As naive as it may sound, I kept seeing little clips in my mind of Humphrey Bogart and Ingrid Bergman in the movie "Casablanca." And just as that story was both romantic and bittersweet, so were the real-life stories I was hearing that night.

CHAPTER 32

August 21, 1941
Casablanca

For their first few weeks in the city of Casablanca, Alfred and Laurette spent much of their time exploring. Although they still had to be cautious of the fascist soldiers posted throughout the city, for the most part they were free to move about as they pleased.

Alfred took many photographs of the city and the desert. He especially enjoyed taking portraits of the people. Even though their religion did not allow them to be photographed, many of the local people were fascinated by Alfred's camera and permitted him to take a few discrete photos.

Through Robert's connections, Alfred was able to get his photographs developed, including the ones he had taken of the French fleet. Robert told Alfred many top-secret military details of the exact location of the ships and the ammunitions storage dumps. Alfred memorized it all, knowing some day this information might come in handy.

As often as he could, Robert joined the couple on their excursions around the city and the neighboring villages and showed them places to dine. He took them to a beautiful beach where they swam in the sea for hours.

One day Laurette and Alfred rented bicycles and rode into Rabat, a small town about 15 kilometers from Casablanca. The sights and sounds captivated Laurette.

"Alfred," she said as they biked to the side of the road, "let's plan to take a trip to Marrakech. I have heard so much about this place and how beautiful it is. Alfred, please...."

Portraits of Moroccan people

"As usual," Laurette thought, "he isn't paying attention to me."

Suddenly she realized that Alfred had leaned way over and nearly toppled off his bike. She quickly helped him sit down under a tree. The heat of the day had apparently caused him to feel light-headed. She fanned his pale face and wiped his brow.

"Alfred, are you all right?"

"It's my throat," he said gruffly. He was clearly in pain.

"It's those tonsils again, isn't it."

"I don't know."

"Open up." Laurette peered in at the back of his throat and saw that it was inflamed and covered with little white spots. She gave him a drink from the canister of water they always carried and slowly helped him back on his feet. "We need to get you back to the hotel," Laurette said.

The couple walked their bicycles slowly back into town and returned them to the rental shop. Alfred was beginning to revive and they decided to stop at a local coffee shop for a cool drink. As they sat under an umbrella sipping lemonade they noticed a familiar couple walking toward them. The man's head was turned distinctly to one side. It was Dr. Costina and his wife! How wonderful to see their friends! Laurette ran up to them and accompanied the couple back to the table.

"How are you and where are you staying and how were you able to get away from the camp?" Laurette was so excited the questions flew out faster than her friends could respond.

"Sit down, sit down. Please join us for a drink and we'll have plenty of time to catch up," said Alfred, always the calm clear thinker.

So the Costina couple sat down and began to describe the hot, filthy, crowded conditions of the camp in the desert. Laurette and Alfred were horrified to think that their fellow travelers had to bear such terrible misfortune.

"But they are surviving and making the best of the situation and living with the intense hope that this will be a short, temporary stay," said Dr. Costina who sounded hopeful himself. "Meanwhile," he went on, "I made connections with several friends of mine in Rabat who found us a very small room about five kilometers from Casablanca. It's very close to a small hospital where I have been helping out. So, here we are!"

"Alfred," said Madame Costina looking concerned, "You appear to be quite pale. Are you all right?"

Alfred began to speak, but Laurette jumped in: "We have just come back from a bicycle ride to Rabat. Alfred nearly passed out in the heat of the sun. It's his tonsils."

Alfred glared at her. "I'll be fine. It was just a touch of heat exhaustion, that's all."

"Let me take a look," Dr. Costina insisted. This was just what Alfred was hoping to avoid.

The doctor looked deep into Alfred's throat. "Alfred, I have told you this before. Those tonsils must come out. I have a place near our room outside of town where I can take care of this for you."

Alfred looked skeptical.

"You will not feel relief until these tonsils are removed. I'll take good care of you, you'll see. Come to this address the day after tomorrow." He was writing an address on a napkin. Alfred was not at all convinced.

"Come on, honey," Laurette insisted, "You will feel so much better." Laurette had great confidence in Dr. Costina and was anxious for her husband to be healthy again before their long voyage.

When Laurette and Alfred arrived at the address Dr. Costina had given them, their hearts sank. It reminded them of the place in Marseilles where Alfred had his tooth extracted, not at all a pleasant memory. And this place was even more primitive. Alfred was feeling some very strong misgivings.

"Come on Alfred. We're here now. And besides," Laurette said, reading his mind, "you survived the tooth extraction in Marseilles and nothing can be as bad as that!" Alfred wasn't so sure.

A moment later, Dr. Costina arrived with his wife as assistant. He had with him a pair of ordinary scissors, which suddenly appeared very menacing to Alfred. From the corner of the room, the doctor brought out a pump. It looked very much like an ordinary bicycle pump, which is exactly what it was.

"I have converted this pump to aspirate instead of pump so it will keep my field clear as I operate," Dr. Costina explained. Alfred understood that this simple device was going to be sucking the blood out of his throat.

Dr. Costina saw that Alfred was growing paler and encouraged him to lie down on the simple bed. The doctor gave him a sedative so he would relax. Then he turned to Laurette.

"You may stay if you like, but this will take some time. I would encourage you to go for a walk and return maybe in an hour and a half. I will take good care of your husband."

Laurette continued to have great confidence in the surgeon. So, as he suggested, she went for a walk while her husband had his operation.

Several hours later, Alfred opened his eyes to find himself in a hospital room surrounded by many other sick people. There were nuns dressed in black attending to the patients, some of whom were moaning with pain. Alfred could barely swallow. At first, all he could think of was the hands of the surgeon in his mouth for hours and hours. He was cutting each vein, and tying a knot, one at a time. Then there was the sound of that bicycle pump, churning away, sucking the blood from his throat as he gagged and choked.

Now, there was just a dull, constant pain. Alfred drifted in and out of consciousness as his wife sat next to him with a cool compress on his forehead. Alfred would open one eye and ask for something to drink. "My mouth is so dry," he whispered, gulping with pain.

"You are only permitted to have a bit of ice," Laurette responded helping him to open his mouth slightly so she could insert a small sliver of ice. She sat with him until it was dark outside and the nuns had come by for the third time to tell her to go home.

"Alfred," she said softly, "I must leave now. But I will be here first thing tomorrow morning."

Laurette left the hospital reluctantly. Alfred looked so weak and pale. There were so many people dying around him. If he could just make it through that night, she would take him back to the hotel as soon as he was strong enough to walk.

Not wanting to be far from her husband's side, Laurette spent the night with a Spanish family that lived near the hospital. She tried to fall asleep, but she was worried about Alfred and she kept feeling the pinching bites of the bedbugs. So she got up and walked around for a while, and finally fell into a restless sleep while sitting in a chair.

Sometime during the night, Alfred awoke coughing and spitting blood. He tried to call out. It seemed like forever before a very young nun came and gave him some ice. But Alfred was sure he needed more than ice. Blood seemed to pour out of him. He felt so weak. The little nun sat with him, giving him ice and trying to make him comfortable. Finally he fell back into a restless sleep.

The next morning, Laurette walked into Alfred's room to find Dr. Costina with his hands inside Alfred's throat, tying off the vein that had opened during the night. His fingers worked quickly. At the same time he scolded the young nun who stood by.

"Why didn't you call me? This man could have bled to death during the night!"

The young nun cowered. Laurette was shocked. She came close and held Alfred's hand as Dr. Costina finished his work and wiped his own hands. The young nun cleaned the blood from Alfred's mouth and then hurried away.

"He'll be fine now," the doctor comforted Laurette. "It was a close call but everything will be all right."

Laurette looked over at her husband who had finally fallen into a restful sleep. His face was a ghostly gray-white. She shivered to think how close she had come to losing him.

After several hours, Alfred awoke and asked for something to drink. He looked and sounded much better. Laurette was greatly relieved. "You gave us quite a scare, Alfred!" she said. He smiled weakly.

Dr. Costina poked his head in the door of the room. "Well, Alfred. How are we feeling today? I've taken one of those nasty tonsils. Pretty soon when you're feeling a little stronger, I'll go in and get the other one."

Although he nodded weakly in response, Alfred made a promise to himself, right then, that he would never let anyone touch his other tonsil!

తతతత

My poor father! He really did suffer physically through this whole ordeal. I had no idea how many times he had stared death in the face. And my mother always had to be strong for both of them. I waited impatiently to hear how they finally managed to cross the Atlantic.

CHAPTER 33

November 16, 1941
Casablanca

It was mid-November and the passengers on the Mont Viso had been in Casablanca for nearly six months. In the weeks after Alfred's tonsil operation, he and Laurette had spent much of their time studying Spanish and English from self-instruction books to prepare for their time in Cuba and America. As Alfred became stronger, he and Laurette were again able to take some day trips, as they had before. Together with Robert they had gotten into all kinds of predicaments. One evening, while they were walking through downtown Casablanca, Robert saw an Arab he didn't like very much. So Robert, just for fun, grabbed a pot of flowers and sneaked up behind the Arab who was seated on a step talking with friends. Robert placed the pot on the Arab's head and ran off laughing while the Arab chased him, screaming in Arabic. Alfred and Laurette were hiding around the corner of a building watching the whole ridiculous show.

On another occasion, Robert was kidding around with one of his seaman friends who dared him to take a whole handful of malaria pills. Robert promptly popped the quinine pills into his mouth and swallowed hard. Within minutes, he had passed out on the floor. Alfred ran next door to find Gary, a big burly fellow who happened to be a German refugee. The two men came back and lifted Robert from the floor. He was heavy, a deadweight and Alfred, who weighed only about 120 pounds, could feel an uncomfortable twinge in his back as he and Gary hoisted their unconscious friend onto the bed. While Alfred quietly rubbed the strained muscle in his back, Laurette sat on the bed next to Robert and stroked his forehead.

"You silly fool," she whispered to her unconscious friend.

Alfred and Laurette spent the night on the floor next to Robert. Laurette woke several times to check if Robert was still breathing. He seemed to be in a very deep sleep.

In the morning, Laurette sat up on the floor feeling stiff and not very well rested. She could see that Robert was beginning to stir.

"Alfred," she said in a hushed tone. "Alfred, wake up."

Her husband began to move slowly and then grabbed his back as he sat up. "I think I pulled something last night," he said cringing slightly.

At that moment, Robert swung his legs over the side of the bed, stood up and stretched as if waking from a particularly restful sleep. "So, what did I miss?" he asked innocently.

Alfred and Laurette rolled their eyes and laughed.

About a week later, Robert knocked on their hotel room door. When he came in, Laurette noticed that he looked uncharacteristically concerned.

"What is it, Robert?" she asked.

"I have some good news and some bad news. The good news is that my roommate is to be released from the hospital in a few days. Laurette and Alfred immediately guessed the bad news. This meant that Robert would need his hotel room once again.

"I have been asking all over town and there aren't any rooms to be found anywhere in Casablanca," Robert went on sadly. "I can't let you two go to that refugee camp now. And besides, there are strong indications that the passage through the Atlantic will open very soon."

"Well then," said Alfred, "Let's go out and start scouring the city for a room. There must be something available somewhere. We don't need much space." He was always the optimist.

So Alfred and Laurette stopped first at the largest hotel in the city. Laurette walked to the front desk, trying to think of something clever to say. The young man at the counter spoke French with a decidedly Belgian accent. He looked familiar to Laurette. Was she imagining things?

"*Voudriez-vous de la'assistance, Madame*? May I help you, Madam?" he asked politely.

"Do you have any rooms?" Laurette asked in the sweetest tone that she could muster, trying not to sound too desperate.

"I am sorry Madam, but we have no rooms." His response was curt. Then he turned his back to the other hotel employees. In a voice barely above a whisper, he said "come back tonight at 10 o'clock."

Laurette nodded her head once to show she understood, then quickly turned back to Alfred. "Come on, let's go. They have nothing."

She was careful not to raise any suspicious looks from the guards at the door or the other employees behind the counter. Despite the relative freedom they had been enjoying in Casablanca these past months, they had always to be conscious of the fascist soldiers and guards there.

Once they were outside and away from the hotel door, Alfred finally felt free to ask. "What else did he say to you?"

"He said to come back tonight at 10 o'clock. Alfred, I swear I have seen this man many times before."

"Oh, you just think so because he has a Belgian accent."

"Well, in any case, I think he will do something for us."

So off they went to try to enjoy the rest of the afternoon, with plans to return to the hotel that evening.

At exactly 10:00 P.M., Alfred and Laurette entered the hotel lobby. They found the young man alone at the counter.

"*Bonsoir, Monsieur,*" Laurette began.

"*Bonsoir. Madame*, I believe I know you. Where are you from?"

"Yes, I believe I know you too! I am from Brussels."

"What part of Brussels?"

"Boitsfort"

"I am also from Boitsfort!" Laurette responded excitedly. "What is your name?"

"Alexander Frankel," responded the young man.

"Frankel! You must be the brother of my friend and schoolmate, Marie Frankel!" Laurette was beginning to remember now.

"Yes, Yes, I have a sister, Marie! I miss her very much."

"Did you take the trolley from Rue du Couloir into the center of town?" Laurette wanted to know.

"Yes I was on that trolley every morning," said Alexander Frankel.

"That is where I remember seeing you!" Laurette felt triumphant, as if she had just completed a difficult jigsaw puzzle.

"I haven't been back to Brussels for two years. I am worried about my family," said Monsieur Frankel sadly.

"I visited with your family before I left Brussels about ten months ago," said Laurette, remembering her frightening night on the couch under the huge framed picture. "They were fine then."

Laurette continued talking with the young man for several minutes. Suddenly Alexander remembered why Laurette had come to the hotel. He looked over at Alfred and then back at Laurette.

"You said you needed a room, didn't you?"

"Yes, my husband and I are desperate for a place to stay. It doesn't have to be much."

"Well, the only thing I have is supposed to be used as a broom closet. But it is large enough to hold a cot. I can put you in there for a while."

And so Alfred and Laurette found themselves a place to stay. It wasn't grand, to be sure, but it saved them from being forced into the refugee camp in the desert.

The next day, they met Robert at the dock. He was looking even more excited than usual. "I have news!" he said. "Come." He walked them to a little tavern by the water. When they were seated he ordered cold drinks. Then he began.

"As you know, there is a Jewish organization that has been working very hard to get a ship to take all of you to your destination. Well, there's a vessel coming in from Portugal the day after tomorrow. It's called the Serpa Pinto. It's a substantial passenger ship, nothing like the freighter you were on. This is the ship that will take you across the Atlantic. Buses have been reserved to bring your fellow travelers from the camp on Tuesday and on Thursday you depart!"

They toasted their voyage. Then Laurette put down her glass and looked sadly at Robert. "This means we will be leaving you." She was unable to hide her emotion.

Robert took her hands in both of his. He looked into her eyes. "Now that some ships can pass, I will also be back on the sea. There is much to do for the war effort. But don't fret my friends, we will keep in touch. We will write. And, who knows when my ship will dock in America! You can't get rid of me that easily!"

The three of them continued for hours to reminisce about their time together and the crazy adventures they had shared.

The next two days passed quickly. Before they knew it, Alfred and Laurette were standing at the docks gazing at the huge ship, the Serpa Pinto, which was to become their home while they crossed the Atlantic. As they were imagining what it would be like to finally be on their way, they began to notice some of their fellow passengers were arriving. From the way their friends looked, Laurette and Alfred could tell that the conditions at the camp had been pretty awful. They were all very thin and many appeared to be weak and sick. Laurette saw her friend Suzy and ran toward her. Suzy had deep circles under her eyes as if she hadn't slept in weeks, and her skin had a tinge of yellow from a bout with hepatitis. But she smiled broadly and gave her friends a big hug.

"Where is Janine?" Laurette asked, looking around.

"Janine is not feeling very well," Suzy said looking terribly worried. "Here she is now." Young Janine walked slowly up to the group, her head lowered and her brow furrowed with pain. The rest of the Hermann family followed close behind.

"My head really hurts," she said softly.

Suzy took her sister's hand and began to walk with her. Alfred and Laurette joined them.

"I think Janine may have eaten some bad chicken she got from a local street vendor the day we were released from the camp. Her stomach was very upset yesterday, and today she has been complaining that her head is hurting." Suzy turned and lifted Janine's chin in her hand. "Once we get on board, you'll be able to lie down, little one," she said.

"Oh, I'll be all right," Janine replied, trying to sound strong. But she could only manage a weak smile as they all boarded the Serpa Pinto together.

The accommodations on this ship were better than the makeshift bunks they had slept on between the cargo holds on the Mont Viso, with cattle and the smell of sulfur. But the Serpa Pinto was also quite crowded and the men ended up sleeping near one of the boiler rooms. The oil smell was almost as noxious as the sulfur had been.

On the last evening before they were to set sail, Alfred and Laurette sneaked over to Robert's ship for one last dinner. It was bittersweet and they hugged each other for a long time.

"I promised you I would write and I will," Robert insisted. "Just be sure to send me your address when you are settled."

He gave the couple his address in Belgium and invited them to visit him and his wife there once the war was over. It was nearly 2 A.M. when Alfred and Laurette finally stepped down from Robert's ship for the very last time. As the rowboat slowly shuttled them back to the Serpa Pinto, they glanced back sadly at the Frederick. They were both going to miss Robert Borrelle, even more than they could imagine.

Though they were filled with sadness to be leaving their friend and their memories in the port of Casablanca, Alfred and Laurette found there was much to keep them distracted as they prepared for departure the next morning. The excitement of the impending voyage was beginning to permeate the atmosphere. By late afternoon, all the passengers had gathered on deck to watch as the ship slowly pulled away from the dock. Laurette waved one last, long goodbye to the Frederick while Alfred took pictures of the scene. A chapter of their lives had ended.

Laurette waves goodbye to the Frederick

Linda Linton

Chapter 34

November 29, 1941
Somewhere on the Atlantic

It had been several days since the Serpa Pinto had left the Port of Casablanca. Alfred was on the upper deck playing chess. In between moves, he reflected on the last few days. When the ship launched, the rocking motion and the smell of the oil in the boiler room had made him instantly seasick. But thankfully, he and most of the others had become accustomed to the movement and the smells and were doing pretty well.

On their second night at sea, one of two women who were both pregnant when they boarded the ship in Casablanca gave birth. There was quite a commotion. The Portuguese physician who was supposed to take care of everyone was so drunk he had no idea the woman was in labor. Fortunately, two of the refugee passengers were doctors and they came to the aid of the pregnant woman. After 13 hours of intense labor, she gave birth to a healthy baby boy. The passengers felt renewed hope with this new life.

Janine was another story completely. What had started as a headache and low-grade fever had become much more serious. She had become steadily weaker and was now refusing to eat anything at all.

At first, the doctor had diagnosed it as malaria (he called it *Paludisme*). It was a logical conclusion to have drawn, considering the conditions she and the other refugees had tolerated in the refugee camp, Sidi El Ayashi, where mosquitoes and bed bugs were everywhere. Suzy had described how the former Legionnaire's camp had been deserted for some time when the group from the Mont Viso arrived. Each of them had to make their beds out of bags of straw and wash everything, including the mosquito nets, in bleach before they could be used. Food was scarce and lavatory conditions were miserable. Some, like Suzy, had contracted hepatitis. Others had severe dysentery.

But Janine had managed to stay reasonably healthy during their time in the camp. Suzy was convinced that it was the chicken from a street vendor in Casablanca that had made Janine ill. Whatever the cause, she had now progressed to purpura fulminante, which meant her blood vessels were weakening and she was developing purple blotches all over her body where the vessels had burst. It was obvious that she needed a blood transfusion.

After questioning all the passengers and finding no one with compatible blood to give to her sister, Suzy had finally found a crewmember with O-negative blood. She knew that this type of blood was known as the "universal donor" type. In the absence of an exact match with her sister's blood type, this O-negative blood would be the least likely type to cause a compatibility problem.

The refugee doctors helped to set up a crude mechanism for transfusion. It had taken several hours to transfuse the blood into the little girl's tiny vein. Slowly, like a parched flower enjoying a warm spring rain, Janine began to revive. Eventually, she was able to sit up on her cot and drink a bit of soup. Her cheeks, which had been sallow and pale for so long, showed a touch of pink. She smiled and a bit of the familiar sparkle shone in her eyes.

"I'm feeling much better," she announced.

Alfred and Laurette were thrilled to see her looking so much better, and Suzy was greatly relieved. Upon Janine's insistence, her family and friends agreed to take her very slowly up to the top deck for some fresh air. Alfred held her by her left arm, while her father walked on her right side, his arm securely about her waist. The passengers on the top deck applauded when they saw her coming. It was quite a scene.

Janine had only the strength to walk a very short distance. Then her father laid her carefully on a lounge chair in the shady part of the deck. She fell asleep almost instantly. Laurette sat with the Hermann family while Alfred went off to engage in a game of chess. In the distance there was the sound of the new baby crying and then cooing softly as he suckled at his mother's breast. It was truly a beautiful day.

Later that evening, when Janine was back on the lower deck, she began to shiver. The pallor was back in her cheeks and her brows were pinched together in a tense look of pain and fear. Suzy called in vain for the ship's doctor, who was swaggering and mumbling and smelling strongly of liquor. Next to Janine, on either side of her bunk, were two adults and one child who had contracted the measles. Their skin was covered with red spots and they perspired heavily with fever.

The two refugee doctors were so busy with the measles outbreak, they had little time for Janine. And with whatever little time they did have, there was not much they could do but try to make her comfortable. It was obvious that one blood transfusion had not been sufficient. The young girl's fever was so high she had begun to hallucinate. Suzy and her family members took turns keeping vigil at Janine's bed for the next two days. They tried to soothe her fever with cool compresses and they forced her to swallow tiny mouthfuls of water to keep her from dehydrating completely. But everyone knew she was not recovering.

Late on the third evening since Janine had taken a turn for the worse, Alfred and Laurette were sitting alone together on the upper deck while Suzy and her family were steadfastly at Janine's side. The girl had lost consciousness that afternoon and had become completely unresponsive. Her breathing was shallow, her heartbeat very faint. Alfred spoke softly to his wife: "I have asked the captain what we will do when Janine dies."

Laurette shuddered and turned away momentarily. She didn't like to even think about this, though she knew it could not be prevented. Alfred continued:

"I have arranged to be there when it is time. I have seen the small coffin they have prepared. I think it is going to happen tonight. I will make sure that everything is taken care of. It will be far too emotional for the family to see. But I wanted you to know that I will be there and everything will be all right."

Alfred slept on the top deck that night so he would be ready. At two o'clock in the morning, he could feel the ship had stopped moving. Janine's breathing had also ceased. Two crewmembers carefully placed her body in a small coffin, draped it with the Portuguese flag and placed it on a sliding board with great care. The captain and several officers stood by and saluted as the flag-draped box slipped down into its final resting place. Then the motors rumbled and the ship continued on its course.

The next morning the captain spoke with the Hermann family and told them exactly where young Janine had been laid to her final rest. It was a very, very sad day. A bright glowing candle had gone out of all their lives.

The Portuguese ship Serpa Pinto

༖ ༖ ༖

How very sad for Aunt Suzy. I knew she'd had a sister, but I didn't know her sister was so young when she died. What a tragedy that Janine had come so close to knowing freedom in America and yet lost her fight for life only days before her family would land on the other side of the Atlantic. The rest of the voyage must have felt so empty for her family and friends.

CHAPTER 35

December 4, 1941
Hamilton Harbor, Bermuda

"It seems like we've been on this boat for months," sighed Laurette, who was missing her friend Robert very much.

"I know," said Suzy. She was still terribly despondent over the loss of her sister. Sometimes she would take out the notebook Janine used to write in and read some of her poetry. Tears dripped down Suzy's cheeks as she read. Together, her friends tried to comfort her by helping her to believe that Janine was now out of pain and watching over them somehow.

Both Suzy and Laurette had been sitting with their eyes closed, lost in their own sad thoughts when Alfred suddenly appeared. He had his camera in hand and appeared particularly pleased about something.

"I was just speaking with the captain," he said animatedly. "We will be landing in Hamilton Harbor in Bermuda this afternoon!"

At that moment, an announcement came over the public address system: "Attention everyone. In one hour we will be arriving in the harbor of Hamilton, Bermuda. Please gather your luggage and assemble on deck in preparation for our landing.

A wave of excitement spread across the ship. "At last!"

The passengers were smiling and chatting merrily as they packed their bags and prepared for arrival in Bermuda.

A short while later, people began to gather on the top deck. They were pointing and exclaiming that they could see land–a welcome sight after many days of viewing only ocean water.

Almost exactly an hour after the announcement of the landing, the ship pulled up to the dock in Hamilton. The excitement among the passengers was pervasive. They gathered in anticipation as the gate opened and seven British Naval officers mounted the ramp to the top deck. They were joined by several members of British Intelligence, and even an inspector from Scotland Yard! The officers carefully began to examine every single piece of luggage. They interviewed each and every passenger, using German, French, and Polish translators.

It took many hours to complete the interrogations. But somehow it was tolerable because, unlike with so many previously harsh inspections they had endured in the past, these refugees realized that the British were not the enemy. Their questioning was firm but kind. They were not accusatory, but rather genuinely concerned. The British wanted to protect themselves from infiltration by spies, yes. But they also wanted to preserve the integrity and honor of their guests. They were well aware of the misery many of these people had endured. And when the whole inspection was over, the officers handed out cigarettes and chocolates and welcomed the passengers with genuine hospitality.

"Chocolates," Laurette whispered with tears of joy and relief glistening in her eyes, "I haven't had a chocolate in such a long time!"

While people were beginning to relax and speak freely again, Alfred reached into a special compartment in his bag, which was miraculously left untouched during the inspection. He drew out his treasured Leica camera and the photographs of the French fleet he had taken just outside the harbor in Casablanca. Quietly, he approached one of the British Naval officers. In the few words he knew in English he managed to say, "Sir, I believe here I have something for you."

The officer's eyes widened. He put a hand on Alfred's shoulder and walked him over to a table where the other officers and inspectors were gathered. He requested a French interpreter and ordered a pot of tea and biscuits. When everyone was comfortable, Alfred opened the pouch containing the precious photographs and began to tell his captivated audience of all the details he had memorized exactly as Robert had told him. People had begun to gather around. The officers were speaking rapidly in English and pointing to particular ships in the photographs and nodding their heads in agreement with one another and approval of their "star witness."

"Go on, please, Monsieur Liebermann." Alfred was surely enjoying the limelight, Laurette observed. And certainly he deserved it.

When he had finished telling everything he knew about the photographs, the British Intelligence agent asked politely if they could keep the photographs, the negatives, the film, and even the camera. He apologized for the inconvenience, but Alfred certainly understood. The officer asked for an address where he might send the photographic equipment when British Intelligence was finished with them. Alfred gave them the only address he had, the address of his parents and brother in Philadelphia, Pennsylvania.

What a magnificent day it had been. The sunset that evening was spectacular. The food was plentiful and delicious. And although they were not permitted to leave the ship, every passenger knew the sweet feeling of freedom.

CHAPTER 36

December 6, 1941
Passing By Islands

The Serpa Pinto was docked only two days in Hamilton Harbor, just long enough to refuel and restock. Then they were off again, this time a fairly short distance to Santo Domingo and Haiti. As they peered over the railing of the top deck, Alfred and Laurette saw, for the first time in their lives, an entire population of jet-black-skinned people. They had read about such places and had seen photographs of some villages in Africa. But this was the first time they had ever seen people who looked so different from themselves, at such a close distance. Their hair was very dark and kinky curly and mostly very long. Many had large noses that flared out and large white teeth.

Alfred longed for his camera. These people were beautiful and he was so eager to take portraits of them. He had borrowed a camera from one friend, but it wasn't nearly so sharp or powerful as his Leica. Besides, the upper deck was simply too far away and anyone who was not planning to immigrate to these island countries was not permitted to leave the ship. This time they were docked for less than a day.

CHAPTER 37

December 7, 1941
The Caribbean Sea, Heading for Cuba

Early on the morning that the Serpa Pinto was to land in Havana, Cuba, word had spread among the passengers that something important had happened in the war that could have a potential impact on the entire world. Many of the passengers gathered around the radio straining to listen to the news. From the little bit of English they understood, they could just barely make out that something significant had occurred in the South Pacific on the island of Hawaii. Then the voice became clear. It was the voice of Franklin D. Roosevelt, President of the United States. The Japanese had bombed Pearl Harbor! The U.S. was being drawn into the war! Now what?

A few hours later, the ship stopped in the water less than three kilometers from the port of Havana. Alfred and Laurette could tell from the comments of some crewmembers that a great argument was brewing on board. Because of the critical world event that had just taken place, the Cuban government wanted to send the Serpa Pinto back to Portugal! They had made it all this way! They were free! And now they were going to be sent back? No! Impossible!

Cuba was the place that their visas were to allow them to enter. They had all the right paperwork! "But the harbor is closed," the authorities were insisting.

And so the negotiations began. There were bitter discussions. Several international and Jewish organizations became involved. After many hours of negotiating, while the passengers stood silently on deck, the ship finally began to move toward the harbor of Havana.

Then, one by one, as each passenger stepped down from the ship, they were loaded onto buses and taken to a place called Triscornia. For Alfred, this felt somewhat like his experience at St. Cyprien, for this too was, in essence, an internment camp. Thankfully, he realized, the conditions were not quite as severe. And although the Cuban people in charge were generally pleasant, they were clearly not intending to let the refugees out of the camp.

A day went by. Then two days. Alfred tried desperately to get a message to his father in Philadelphia. Since everyone else in his family had gotten to the U.S. from Cuba, surely Alfred's father would be able to find the contacts to free them. But Alfred had no idea whether his messages were getting through.

Meanwhile, several of the other refugees were able to pay their way out. The rumors were that it cost $2,000 in American money to buy freedom for one person. Only a couple of families were allowed to go free. After two days, when no one else could pay that much, the number was said to have dropped to $1,000. Then a few more families were allowed to leave. Several days later, the cost was down to $500.

Ten days after they landed in Cuba, Alfred and Laurette were sitting in their small cubicle in Triscornia. They were drinking a glass of cold fresh milk, a treat they hadn't had in a very long time. It tasted delicious! They were talking with the Altmanns, an older couple they'd befriended. One day Laurette had jokingly called the gentleman "Papa" and he enjoyed the endearment. So from that time on, Laurette and Alfred had called the couple Mama and Papa Altmann.

As they sat with the Altmanns and enjoyed their milk, a young messenger boy walked over to Alfred. "Excuse *Señor*, for you," he said in Spanish and in English as he handed an envelope to Alfred. Laurette smiled at the funny sound of two languages she barely understood.

Alfred's eyes opened wider as he examined the envelope. It was from his father! The note had come through a woman who knew the Cuban President, Batista. The woman, an underground contact whom Alfred's father had managed to reach, also happened to be the daughter of the cousin of Mama and Papa Altmann. What a small world!

Alfred opened the letter to find there was money inside. The amount was sufficient to pay their way out of the camp (the cost had now dropped to $200) with enough left to give them a start in Cuba.

When arrangements were made for their release from camp, Alfred and Laurette were pleased to learn they were to move out the same day as Mama and Papa Altmann. They were to be joined by another couple from Austria and a single girl who was originally from France. There were not many available options for living quarters in Havana at the time. So all seven of them were set up, temporarily, in a boardinghouse where many of the other refugees were staying.

This boardinghouse smelled awful. It was filthy, with rats and roaches scrambling across the floor at night. Rumors of infiltrators, Nazi spies living among them, were rampant. During many long nights, screams could be heard coming from several floors away. After three days, Laurette couldn't stand the place a moment longer. Fortunately, Alfred was able to find another boardinghouse, owned by a woman and her son. Alfred not only arranged to move himself and Laurette to this new location, he even managed to have the Altmanns join them along with the Austrian couple and the French woman. By this time they had all become good friends.

Their new boardinghouse arrangements were much cleaner. There were no rats and Laurette noticed only a few roaches. She and Alfred began to feel somewhat more comfortable. Together with the Altmanns, the young Austrian couple and the French girl, they began to establish themselves and plan for their future journey to the United States. But it wasn't easy.

The Liebermanns and their friends learned very quickly that the only way to get anything done, whether to obtain letters at the post office, or to send a telegram or even to find a job, they had to know "the right guys." Everyone had to have "a connection." And of course the refugees had to pay one of these "guys" each time something was needed, even if it was just to receive their own mail! And whatever was paid to this guy, he would, in turn, split with the people in the post office. It was terribly corrupt.

In addition, once a week, each of the refugees had to report to the police. There, the official would open the individual's file and he or she had to drop in one U.S. dollar. That file, Alfred was to learn, would go into a drawer and eventually the money would be split with President Batista. So, in this way, every refugee or immigrant that came into Cuba contributed to the wealth of the Cuban president. It was a sickening way to live, but the Liebermanns did what they had to do to survive.

As days and weeks went by, Alfred and Laurette began to feel more comfortable with their surroundings. Thanks to their self-study in Casablanca, they were quickly learning to speak Spanish, which was helping them to meet people and begin to find employment.

One day, through a friend of Mama Altmann, Laurette learned of a Cuban family that was looking for a French governess for their children for a few weeks. This was a welcome opportunity, since refugees were not permitted to work for any Cuban companies.

And what a challenge it turned out to be for Laurette! Thank goodness she had a good ear for languages and she was picking up many more Spanish words and phrases very quickly. But most of the time she spent reading French storybooks to the children. It was an amusing adventure, and what was more important, it brought in a little bit of badly needed money.

Meanwhile, Alfred had managed to purchase a used camera and had met a very nice young man named Heinz, from southern Germany, who had agreed to open up a photographic studio with Alfred. Together the two men rented a room they set up as a darkroom. Alfred spent many long hours in that hot room, stripped to the waist with a bandanna around his head to catch the sweat. It was hard, hard work and the pay was minimal, but Alfred loved every minute of it. Together with Heinz he was making important connections and taking some wonderful portraits.

One day, Heinz brought Alfred to visit a refugee friend of his who was a diamond cutter. He had learned the trade in Holland, and had managed to start a diamond-cutting business in Cuba along with several other refugees. The friend gave Alfred and Heinz a tour of the diamond-cutting facility and Alfred was fascinated. He began to take pictures, being very careful not to disturb the workers or to bring any attention to himself and Heinz.

For the next several days, Alfred and Heinz developed those pictures. They worked with the contrast and the sharpness. They cropped the best pictures and took a sample to show Heinz's friend. The friend showed his boss, who came stomping angrily out of his office yelling obscenities about secrets of the diamond-cutting process and shouting, "how dare they take unauthorized photographs."

Fortunately, Alfred had taken an excellent portrait of the boss, and as he showed the man his own likeness, his anger quieted. He suddenly became very interested. He looked sharply at Alfred and Heinz, then back at the photographs.

"Wait here," he said and he disappeared into a stairwell.

Heinz's friend was as perplexed and worried as the photographers. Moments later, the boss returned with the owner of the diamond-cutting operation!

"Who took these photographs?" the owner wanted to know.

"I did," Alfred said, trying to sound confident despite his sweating palms and dry mouth.

Suddenly the man smiled. "They are quite good," he said. "Can you do more of them?"

"Of course," Alfred and Heinz said almost simultaneously.

"I would like you to do a complete photo story of my facility. You will have full opportunity to photograph all the steps in the diamond-cutting process."

Alfred, who moments earlier had begun to experience that all-too-familiar feeling that he was going to pass out, was now shaking the boss's hand with enthusiasm. The color had returned to his cheeks and his heart was racing.

"Yes, of course. We will be honored to photograph your facility. I know you will be very pleased with the results."

Alfred practically flew home to tell Laurette the news. What an opportunity this would be! He couldn't wait to begin!

When he arrived at the boardinghouse, Laurette was there to greet him with her own news. Now she was the one who was looking quite pale.

"Laurette, what is it," Alfred asked, "are you sick?"

"Not exactly." she replied abruptly

"What is it, then?"

"I think I might be pregnant."

Alfred gazed at her in stunned disbelief. This he hadn't anticipated at all. His own light-headed dizziness was returning. He walked her to their small couch and they both sat down. He looked at her for a long moment.

"Are you sure?"

"Well, I went to the doctor today. He is doing some tests and we will know for certain in a few days. I had a serious talk with this doctor. You remember, the one who took care of my appendix several months ago? He asked if we were prepared to have a baby right now. He said he believes that every child has the right to be wanted. If we're not ready to have a child at this time, this doctor will help us. He will perform a safe abortion right away. Alfred, what do you think?"

"You know I have always wanted children," Alfred said gently. "But we can't afford a baby right now. I know we will be in America soon and then we can begin to have a family. But...."

"I know, I know. Not now. I agree." Laurette looked away.

Alfred turned her face toward him. "I think this is not the time for us to have a baby. We don't have a real home. We have very little money. I don't want to raise a child here in Cuba."

They sat in silence for a long time. Then Alfred broke the somber mood.

"We don't have to make that decision yet until we know for sure." Laurette nodded.

"Now, would you like to hear about my day?" With that opening, Alfred proceeded to tell his wife about the diamond cutters and his new project. Laurette hadn't seen him so excited about anything since before they had left Casablanca.

The next day, Alfred set out to begin his new project and Laurette prepared to finish her job as governess of the Cuban children. There were only a few days left in their original agreement.

Within a few days, Laurette learned that she wasn't pregnant after all. Both she and

Alfred were relieved. Now they would be able to wait until they were settled in America before they would begin thinking about expanding their family.

A month later, after he'd completed his project, Alfred's photographs of the diamond cutters appeared as a "reportage" in the newspaper. Everyone was complimenting the wonderful job he and Heinz had done. And they received a decent sum of money for their work as well.

Meanwhile, Laurette had heard of an American family who had become Cuban citizens and were looking for a French governess for their three young boys. "Well, wouldn't that be interesting," she thought. "I can't speak English and they can't speak French. Thank goodness I know enough Spanish now. At least we would have one language in common!"

Laurette got the job the same day she applied and immediately began to teach the three little boys some French songs and nursery rhymes. Little did she know that she would probably learn much more English from them than they would learn French from her!

Meanwhile, Alfred continued with his photography. He was enjoying the work, but the income was sporadic.

One day, a rather distinguished-looking man with a mustache came into the photo studio. He was wearing a very expensive, well-tailored suit and a handsome hat, which was tipped ever so slightly to one side. He had a cigar in his mouth that he removed with his left hand as he extended his right in a gesture of introduction.

He said his name so quickly in a heavy Cuban-Spanish accent that Alfred didn't quite catch it. What Alfred was able to understand, though just barely, was that this gentleman had seen the small advertisement that Alfred and his partner had put in the local paper. The man was apparently very interested in having some portraits taken. Alfred began to show his potential customer some samples of the work they had done. The *señor* appeared to be impressed as he carefully held one particular portrait of a woman. He also seemed interested in some of Alfred's photographs of the diamond factory.

With his broken Spanish, Alfred was able to determine that the gentleman was interested in having the partners come to an apartment to take some photographs. The man gave Alfred his card. He looked at it carefully. It read simply "Señor M. Martinez." Señor Martinez spoke very slowly so Alfred would be certain to understand every word. He explained that he wanted the photographers to meet him in exactly one week at the apartment location he had handwritten on the card. Then he wrote a number on the back of the card, the price he was willing to pay for the work he wanted Alfred to do. It was a considerable sum of money! Alfred shook the man's hand and agreed to meet him.

Alfred was elated as he headed back to the boardinghouse. There he found Papa Altmann and immediately showed him the business card with great pride. Papa Altmann looked suspicious.

"I know this name, but I am not sure who he is. What is it he has asked you to do for this sum?"

"I will be taking photographs of an apartment. That was as much as I could understand." Alfred was beginning to realize that he could be in danger.

He soon discovered that this man was running an illegal business manufacturing condoms, which were against the law in Cuba! He had become extremely wealthy in this illicit business. It was well known that this man's wife was quite ill and that the wealthy Cuban had a beautiful mistress.

Alfred decided he would not tell Laurette about his new assignment. There was no need to worry her unnecessarily.

The following Thursday, Alfred and Heinz prepared all their equipment and met at the appointed address. The wealthy Cuban opened the door to the magnificent apartment and introduced the photographers to his mistress. The woman was stunning. She was very petite with long black hair and huge beautiful brown eyes with long dark lashes that curved up just at the very tips. It made her eyes appear to flutter in a sort of coquettish way.

Soon it was clear that the wealthy Cuban wanted everything to be photographed, including the young woman. So Alfred and Heinz got to work. They set up each photograph with great care. The place was extraordinary, almost like a museum. And the young woman was quite natural in front of the camera.

It took three hours to complete the shoot and nearly two days to develop all the film. But when they were finished, Alfred and Heinz had a collection of prints they were very proud of. And the wealthy Cuban, true to his word, paid them the sum he had promised, with an extra bonus for a few enlargements of the photos of his mistress.

When Alfred finally told Laurette what he had been working on, she laughed. Why had he been afraid to tell her? Then she paused and began to think of the possible danger of working with a man whose money was obtained illegally. Or was Alfred afraid that Laurette would be jealous?

"We have been through an awful lot together, Alfred," she mused. "Somehow, infidelity is just not one of the things I worry about with you!"

Laurette never completely understood why she felt this way, but Alfred assured her she was absolutely right.

CHAPTER 38

July 29, 1943
Leaving Havana

Almost 20 months had passed since Alfred and Laurette had arrived in Cuba. It was nearly August. Alfred had been getting some frustrating letters from home. His brother-in-law John had been negotiating back and forth with lawyers and officials in Washington, DC, and several government institutions in New York, trying to obtain visas to the U.S. for Alfred and Laurette. It seemed that the State Department was giving them a difficult time because officials mistakenly believed that the social democratic youth organizations, the *Rote Falken* and *Les Faucons Rouges* (the "Red Falcons"), were somehow Communist. Back and forth the argument kept going. Even though John had many influential friends trying to help, he had run into a stalemate over this issue. After all the money that was spent and all the hardships they had endured, it seemed preposterous to Alfred and Laurette that they should be refused entry into the United States over such a ridiculous misunderstanding.

Then one day, unexpectedly, a package arrived.

"Enclosed are your visas, at long last! I will tell you the whole story when I see you," wrote John. "But suffice it to say that the renowned CBS correspondent and journalist, William Shirer, testified in your behalf that the "Red Falcons" is nothing more than a coed Boy Scout organization. He also said that the Social Democrats are just that, democratic, and they have nothing whatsoever to do with Communism. And by a private act in Congress and the signature of President Roosevelt, you have finally received your long-overdue visas! *Bon voyage!*"

"I'll tell you the whole story when I see you…." Alfred read aloud. "How strange and wonderful it is to imagine that we will be seeing them all in a matter of weeks!"

Alfred kissed Laurette and she hugged him for a long time. They couldn't believe it!

After more than three years of fleeing, they were finally "going home" to America!

The arrangements were made very quickly. Alfred's father had sent extra money for the airplane tickets. The couple was to fly into Miami and then take the train to Philadelphia.

Laurette set about selling many of the belongings they didn't expect to need in their new home. She amazed herself when she realized how many friendships they had developed and how fluent in Spanish she and Alfred had become. Their English, however, still left a great deal to be desired.

Alfred helped Heinz prepare to take over the photography business by himself. They had done well together and Alfred was going to miss him.

Heinz accompanied Alfred and Laurette to the airport. (They had already said their tearful goodbyes to Mama and Papa Altmann and they couldn't stand the thought of going through that again.) When all of their remaining belongings were safely checked in and they were about ready to board the airplane, Heinz removed an envelope from his pocket.

"Look, I have a letter here from somebody in Cuba. He wants you to take it to Miami and mail it. He can't send it through the mail here because all the letters are opened by the censors."

Alfred didn't think much about it and tucked the letter into his jacket. Then he gave his friend one last hug, Laurette kissed him on alternate cheeks, and they boarded the airplane for Miami.

CHAPTER 39

August 13, 1943
Miami, Florida, USA

When the plane touched down in Miami, Alfred and Laurette held hands. Miami! They could hardly believe it. Just one more leg of their long journey and they would be reunited with Alfred's family.

As they left the plane, each passenger was carefully searched and then allowed to pass. The inspector searching Alfred found the letter in his pocket. Suddenly his whole manner changed. He yanked Alfred and Laurette aside and they soon found themselves in the company of three FBI agents and on their way to a Coast Guard internment camp.

"Oh no, not again!" Laurette couldn't keep from crying out in fear and frustration. "What is it they want now?

Alfred had a feeling it had something to do with that letter but he had no idea what it was.

When they arrived at the camp, they were strip-searched and interrogated for several hours. Laurette was placed in one small room all alone. Alfred ended up in a cell with a Japanese man who, during this time of the war, was truly considered the enemy. Alfred thought to himself, "Here I am, peacefully trying to join my family and start a new life and now I am being treated like an enemy! And I have no idea why!"

Several days passed. Each day, the same three FBI agents would take Alfred and Laurette out in a limousine to get some food at a local restaurant.

"Mr. and Mrs. Liebermann!" they would shout. Then they would escort the couple to the limousine. The FBI agents would arrange themselves with one agent sitting between the couple and the other two in the front seat.

Each time, upon their return to camp, the agents would interrogate their "prisoners" with the same questions, over and over again. And the answers were always the same.

After three or four days, the security became more lax. Alfred was permitted to play chess with one of the other prisoners. Alfred learned that his chess partner was a rather famous German carmaker who had come to Miami on business. They were holding him at the Coast Guard camp, more or less for his own protection. His wife was there with him and the two couples became quite friendly.

Another two days passed, and now there were only two FBI agents escorting Alfred and Laurette out to get their meals. Still, they continued with the same questioning. And the answers were always the same.

Finally, after ten days, one of the agents came into the holding area.

"Mr. and Mrs. Liebermann," came the usual commanding voice. Then it was punctuated with "you are free to go!"

Alfred and Laurette had no idea why they had been held, nor did they understand why they were being freed. Suddenly, the agent tapped Alfred on the shoulder and said "good luck, Al."

"Al?" Alfred thought to himself. He had never heard his name pronounced that way before, Al. But he liked the sound of it. Very American. Of course Laurette then wanted to "Americanize" her name, too.

So that afternoon, "Loretta" and "Al" boarded the Silver Meteor train from Miami to New York, with a very important stop in Philadelphia. They were finally going home.

CHAPTER 40

August 24, 1943
Philadelphia, Pennsylvania, USA

As the train pulled into the station at 30th Street, Philadelphia, Laurette's heart began to pound. She had been so excited, she hadn't thought about how far from "home" in Brussels she and Alfred had traveled. They had been to France and Morocco and Cuba. It had been like a wonderful and horrible dream. And now, more than three years later, they would be united with Alfred's family.

The train bumped and groaned as they rolled slowly past the onlookers on the platform outside the window. Alfred pressed his forehead to the glass, straining for the sight of a familiar face. And then he saw someone. It was almost like looking into a mirror. It was his brother, Otto! And there was Erna, smiling and waving. Alfred had nearly forgotten how tiny she was, standing next to her husband, John. Ah yes, John Hirschfeld, the one who had persistently contacted every lawyer and government official he could in the effort to bring Laurette and Alfred to America. John walked toward the end of the platform as Alfred and Laurette pressed through the crowd. Their pace quickened. And then the couple saw that familiar smile.

"I see Papa!" Laurette said breathlessly, stumbling toward her husband's family. The couple became enfolded by hugs and laughter and tears, all at the same time. Everyone was trying to speak at once. Most of it was in German, with some English mixed in. Laurette could barely understand what anyone was saying. She turned to Alfred for help and found him snuggled in his mother's arms.

"Mama," Alfred breathed into his mother's ear as she held him tightly. Mama reached out one arm and drew Laurette to her breast as well. Despite the Viennese German accent, Laurette understood the few English words she spoke.

"Welcome home, my children."

Linda Linton

Postscript

Shortly after arriving in Philadelphia, Alfred (Al, to his business associates and Freddy to his friends and family) entered the U.S. Army. He then became a United States citizen and, together with his brother, Otto, changed the family name to Linton. Loretta became a U.S. citizen shortly afterward.

While Alfred was away at boot camp, a high-ranking naval officer came to draft him for a special mission. Perhaps it had something to do with those pictures he took of the French fleet. But it was too late. By the time the officer reached the camp where he had been training, Alfred had already been transferred to the Signal Corps in a different part of the country. So he remained in the Army until he received a hardship leave and later an honorable discharge when his mother died.

Once the war ended, Alfred and Loretta Linton worked hard for many years building a life together in their new home. Al established himself in a successful sales career while Loretta ran the household in a quiet suburb of Philadelphia where they had purchased a house. Together they raised three typical American children who went on to give them four typical American grandchildren.

And none of the children or grandchildren knew the story of how Alfred and Laurette Liebermann fled from Europe and came to America during the war, until a very special 50th wedding anniversary celebration in Bermuda.

I am very grateful to have been a part of what must have been a catharsis for my parents after holding so much inside all those years. These revelations left me with a new appreciation and closeness to my entire family and a particular gratitude to my late Uncle John who, together with my Grandpop, worked so tirelessly to obtain the papers that permitted my parents to enter this country. And I now know that if just one of the many "close calls" had gone differently during my parent's escape from Europe, none of us would be alive today.

Printed in the United States
by Baker & Taylor Publisher Services